Twayne's United States Authors Series

Sylvia E. Bowman, *Editor*

INDIANA UNIVERSITY

Theodore Parker

Theodore Parker

By ROBERT C. ALBRECHT

University of Oregon

Twayne Publishers, Inc.   ::   New York

For Eric

Preface

"The religion I preach will be the religion of enlightened men for the next thousand years" is an immodest statement made by Theodore Parker. Though remembered as a leading Transcendentalist and Abolitionist rather than as the originator of a new religion, he had intended to found a form of liberal Christianity called "absolute religion" that would become the dominant one in a future United States that he described as an industrial democracy. While his life and work might seem to have more variety than unity, Theodore Parker's sermons, lectures, and books—all his efforts—were directed toward the future. Writing of future Christs and of the industrial democracy to come, working for a nation without slavery, preaching a religion not widely accepted, promulgating a method of theological scholarship not welcomed by American theologians, Theodore Parker revealed his utopian vision. But the utopia was not in the life hereafter or in the millennium which would finally come on earth; it was in the foreseeable future that he himself might live to see. Believing in the perfectibility of man and community, Parker devoted his life to bringing about that perfection.

This nineteenth-century preacher who tried to moralize the nation in order to elevate it for its task believed that the heart and soul of the republic lay in New England. He wished to convert the South and paid little attention to the West, but he was not parochial. To have called him the "preaching conscience of the nation" would have delighted him. That he was a great preacher there is no doubt, and that he spoke always and only with self-righteousness even his enemies would admit.

Looking back and forth between the religious principles in which he believed and the conditions of the city and nation he saw around him, he spoke to individuals to follow the dictates of truth which each man could reach through intuition. He was a Transcendentalist who could not rest until he had carried every truth he found to the people in the marketplace. In speech and in action Parker's stance was argumentative. Quite consciously he employed varieties of induction, deduction, and analogy to persuade others of the truths they could find; and he wondered that they were not convinced. He knew and relied on reason and intuition; however, Parker usually ignored the rhetorical modes of persuasion. In his righteousness he would not bend to an audience; he argued in the same way to North and South, congregation and public, Boston and Illinois.

To his contemporaries Parker occupied a radical position in politics, religion, and social reform. Yet he was not one of those radicals who becomes the conservative of the next generation. Rather, Theodore Parker can now be seen as a kind of middle figure: he bridges the Unitarianism of the early nineteenth century and the free religion of the end of the century. He saw the possibility of a capitalism which ground working men into poverty and the idealism of a utopian equality; but since he could accept neither, he believed the best system to be an industrial democracy. None of his contemporaries would call him a moderate, but today he can be seen as one who occupies an historically moderate ideological position. To know Parker's work is to know the central political, social, and religious conflicts of the crucial period of his century during which the nation bled to find its shape and direction. Parker, who understood the tensions within the culture better than most men, tried to turn it toward his vision of perfection.

With such views in mind I have tried to present a critical study of Parker's work. Various aspects of his personal life—his recurrent depression, the quality of his friendship, his relations with his wife, his desire for martyrdom—would be inappropriate subjects. The works discussed are those which most clearly demonstrate his religious, social, political, and moral positions. In many sections I have attempted to give the reader a sense of immediacy in these century-old events. Through his presence and his writings Parker challenged the nation to become what its ideals and his righteousness demanded.

I am grateful to the staffs of the following libraries: Boston Public Library, Massachusetts Historical Society Library, University of Minnesota Library, The University of Chicago Library, Houghton Library of Harvard University, Henry E. Huntington Library, Newberry Library. Special mention must be made of the

Preface

generous courtesies extended by Dr. Margaret Boell of the
Meadville Theological School Library. Mrs. Gloria Principali
and Mrs. Julie Zahn patiently transcribed drafts into typescript.
I wish also to thank those who kindly read parts of the manuscript—John Cawelti of The University of Chicago and Robert
Merideth of Miami University. Charles H. Foster of the University of Minnesota introduced me to the work of Theodore
Parker, provoked my interest, and encouraged me in this and
much other work.

ROBERT C. ALBRECHT

University of Oregon

Contents

Chronology

1810 Theodore Parker born August 24 in Lexington, Massachusetts.
1827 Began several years of school teaching.
1830 Enrolled in Harvard College.
1831 Left home to teach school in Boston.
1832 Opened school in Watertown where he met Convers Francis.
1834 Entered Harvard Divinity School in April.
1835 Edited the *Scriptural Interpreter* for two years while a student.
1837 June 21, ordained at the Spring Street Church in West Roxbury.
1840 Published the Levi Blodgett Letter.
1840 Contributed to *The Dial* for the four years of its existence.
1841 May 19, delivered "A Discourse on the Transient and the Permanent in Christianity."
1841 Winter, gave first lecture series in Boston.
1842 *A Discourse of Matters Pertaining to Religion.*
1843 *A Critical and Historical Introduction to the Canonical Scriptures of the Old Testament.*
1843 September 9, sailed for Europe for a year's absence.
1845 February 16, delivered first sermon in the Melodeon.
1847 Moved to Boston.
1848 Edited the *Massachusetts Quarterly Review* for three years.
1848 *A Letter on Slavery.*
1852 The rendition of Thomas Sims.
1852 Twenty-eighth Congregational Society moved to the Music Hall.

1853   *Sermons of Theism, Atheism and the Popular Theology.*
1854   Rendition of Anthony Burns.
1855   Published his *Defence.*
1859   January 2, preached his last sermon; February 13, left the United States; April 19, finished "Theodore Parker's Experience as a Minister"; October, arrived in Rome.
1860   May 10, died in Rome.

CHAPTER 1

Beginnings and Education

I *Heritage*

W hen Theodore Parker lived in Boston, two firearms hung in his study. These were his inheritance from his grandfather, John Parker, who had carried one into the battle of Lexington on April 19, 1775, and who had captured the other on the same occasion. Theodore Parker consciously felt his inheritance from this man who had led the Americans in the first battle of the Revolutionary War. Commanding the Lexington company, John Parker supposedly had said, "Don't fire unless fired upon; but if they mean to have a war, *let it begin here!*" and the war did begin there. The Minute Men were forced to retreat, but they harassed the British on their way back to Boston. Parker knew the history of that day well and in effect imitated it many times. Often he did not wait to be fired upon; in theology and in social reform, he was more often the aggressor.

Keeping the firearms where he could always see them reminded Parker of the family heritage and especially of the grandfather who had been at Lexington. His first American ancestor, Thomas Parker, had left England in 1635 and settled in Lynn, Massachusetts. Since all remained in eastern Massachusetts, Theodore Parker's family was very much a New England one. While Parker himself had a strong national pride, his affection for his state was exceptionally strong. Every member of the paternal line, except his father, had occupied a position of some importance in the town in which he lived. His father, John Parker, did not hold any local offices and did not own the house in which he lived. Although Parker never commented directly on these matters, he clearly wished in his very ambitious way to surpass his father.

His memories of his father were vague, although he recalled that John Parker read history, political science, mathematics, biography, travels, novels, philosophy, and theology. "He read much on Sundays, in the long winter evenings, sometimes in the winter mornings before it was light, and in the other intervals of toil."[1] Though the elder Parker might have been familiar with much of the range of current literature, his son recalled nothing about his ideas. But the father transmitted to the son a love of learning which never flagged. Parker judged that, since his father's vocations of farmer and mechanic led him away from reading, he himself would combine vocation and reading in a fashion his father did not. But the relations between the father and the son must not have been altogether happy; for, just after his father's death in 1836, when Parker wrote to Lydia Cabot, who was soon to be his wife, a formal, strained, self-pitying letter with comments appropriate to a funeral sermon, he commanded Lydia never again to speak of his father's death.

II   *Childhood*

"On the 24th of August, 1810, early on a hot, sweltering morning, I came into this world of joys and sorrows." So Parker began the section of his autobiography, "From Birth Till the Age of Eight." The tenth child had been born four years before. There was little wealth in the large family, and the riches Parker remembered in 1859 were the hills, orchards, plants and shrubs— the "material surroundings" of his boyhood: "From the middle of May when the introduced trees, the plum, peach, cherry, apple, and pear, began to bloom, till the middle or end of October, the eye need not seek a landscape of humble, quiet New England beauty more attractive than this, and all winter long the white pines, which seemed so cool and attractive in July and August, had a warm, motherly look, and told of life still sleeping in them, around them, everywhere."[2] The scene is an idyllic one that the boy who had grown old remembered. In all his stories and remembrances nothing breaks the stillness and quietude of those early years.

Parker's early accomplishments reveal the drive and ambition he was to exhibit throughout his life. By the time he was eight, after only four short terms in school, he had read Homer and Plutarch; and he was already known as one of the most voracious readers in Lexington. He later recalled that during his first years in school he studied the *New England Primer* from which he derived his first notions of God, Satan, and eternal damnation. No doubt many of his contemporaries retained these ideas for life, but Parker would shed them before he entered the ministry. His preparation for that vocation started when he was ten years old as he began the study of Latin and Greek. A year later he was ready to read Vergil and Cicero, and to begin to study by himself natural philosophy, astronomy, chemistry, and rhetoric.

By eight, Parker was writing poetry, a habit he continued throughout his life. By ten, he could memorize poems of five hundred to one thousand lines after one reading; he remembered after one hearing songs and hymns. His memory was exercised by a scheme his parents used. After he had read a book, they examined him on his reading. If he did not know it well, he was expected to reread it. Such was the preparation of the future scholar who eventually owned thousands of books. In 1822 he bought his first book, a Latin dictionary, purchased with money earned by selling whortleberries in Boston.

III *Teaching*

When he was seventeen, Parker began his short career in teaching. For four years he taught in various towns in the area during the winter term. Apparently he was exceedingly strict and expected a great deal from his pupils. Certainly a boy with such a prodigious memory might well have been too demanding. During the summer of 1830, about the time of his twentieth birthday, perhaps because of some events which occurred in Concord during the previous winter or perhaps because of new stirrings of ambition, he walked to Cambridge to enroll at Harvard. Never residing in Cambridge, he yet finished his work but received no degree because he could not pay the fees for the four years. (The master of arts degree was conferred on him, *honoris causa,* in 1840.) Whatever effect these first years in Cambridge had was surely slight. If he had been able to live in Cambridge, Parker might have then been introduced to Boston and Bostonians.

On March 23, 1831, a year after enrolling at Harvard, Parker went to Boston as an assistant teacher in a private school; and he never returned home except for brief visits. Before him.lay the completion of home studies for his Harvard courses, the teaching in schools, and eventually the work in the Divinity School which was to train him only in a fashion for the work of his life. In 1860, shortly before his death, he recalled his teaching in a letter to Dr. S. G. Howe:

It is twenty-nine years to-day since I left my father's house and home and sought a new in Boston. A raw boy, with clothes made by country tailors, coarse shoes, great hands, red lips, and blue eyes, I went to serve in a private school, where, for fifteen dollars a month and my board, I taught Latin, Greek, subsequently French (!), and Spanish—both which I could read and write, though not speak—the mathematics, and all sorts of philosophy. I was not twenty-one, and hired a man for eleven dollars a month to take my place for five months at home and do the farm work. My father refused to accept this, but I insisted that it would be unjust to use me better than the other boys before me. I taught in the school six hours a day, and from May to September seven; but I always had from ten to twelve hours a day for my own private studies out of school. You may judge what sort of boy I was from the kind of man you have known since. Life lay before me then (it is all behind me now), and I had hope where now is only remembrance. Judge if I did not work: it makes my flesh creep to think how I used to work, and how much I learned that year, and the four next. Had not I a constitution for a scholar? Oh, that I had known the art of life, or found some book or some man to tell me how to *live,* to *study,* to *take exercise,* &c. But I found none, and so here I am.[3]

Parker had come to the great world of Boston, the capital of the world to this rural New Englander; but he learned little of it. Instead, he buried himself in work, although, as he confesses in the letter, he did not know how to achieve self-satisfaction even in his work. Parker was always rightly proud of his prodigious efforts, but, in this last year of his life when he wrote this letter, he correctly judged his inability to know how to live. He put his effort into the task of learning, but later his focus shifted to other kinds of work that were also done with all his energy. Ironically, it was not the learning which caused him to be one of the leading clergymen in the nation. His reputation as a scholar and theologian never equaled his achievements as a preacher and reformer.

This first period in Boston lasted only a year, but it was one filled with long hours of study and of hearing Lyman Beecher preach. Parker's description of this period was recorded in 1859:

For a year, though born and bred among Unitarians, I had attended the preachings of Dr. Lyman Beecher, the most powerful orthodox minister in New England, then in the full blaze of his talents and reputation, and stirred also with polemic zeal against "Unitarians, Universalists, Papists, and Infidels." I went through one of his "protracted meetings," listening to the firey words of excited men, and hearing the most frightful doctrines set forth in sermon, song, and prayer. I greatly respected the talents, the zeal, and the enterprise of that able man, who certainly taught me much; but I came away with no confidence in his theology. The better I understood it, the more self-contradictory, unnatural, and hateful did it seem. A year of his preaching about finished all my respects for the Calvinistic scheme of theology.[4]

Parker makes no attempt to recapture his actual feelings and thoughts while hearing Beecher preach, and it is unlikely that he so clearly saw then his opinions of the theology which he later dismissed as he worked more directly against the Unitarians. He might well have experienced some confusion as he thought over the Unitarian and Calvinistic doctrines which he was beginning to examine. Certainly learning how to attack the Unitarians was an important part of his experience in hearing Beecher. Though Parker soon attacked them from a position quite different from Beecher's, some of his arguments were taken from the long dialogue which took place between the nineteenth-century Calvinists and their Unitarian opponents. Furthermore, Parker's recognition of the talents of Beecher as a preacher suggests that it was during this period that he began to develop his own ideas about preaching, though he never became known for the polemic style of his delivery from the platform or from the pulpit.

The limited worth of the short Boston experience contrasts sharply with the following years spent in Watertown where Parker opened his own school. With respect to his future career as an Abolitionist, the most remarkable event of this period of teaching was his being forced by the protests of white parents to dismiss a Negro girl from the school. He easily submitted to the pressure though he unceasingly regretted his compliance in later years. During his two-year stay in Watertown he met the Unitarian minister Convers Francis, who introduced him to the new Transcendentalist thought and to German scholarship in theology. Francis, the first scholar of theology Parker had met, knew Latin, Greek, Hebrew, and German; and he owned a large library of German books at a time when few were to be found in any American library. Doubtless Convers Francis was in part responsible for Parker's decision to enter the Harvard Divinity School after two years in Watertown. Furthermore, Francis must have shown the younger man *An Appeal in Favor of That Class*

of Citizens Known as Africans, the work of his sister, Lydia
Maria Child. Published in 1833, the pamphlet converted Thomas
Wentworth Higginson and Charles Sumner to antislavery. Perhaps
Parker's name should be added to the list of Abolitionists con-
verted by that book.

As a teacher in the Sunday school of Francis's church, Parker
met another teacher, Lydia Cabot, to whom he became engaged
in 1833 and married in 1837. Important for his scholarly work
was his reading of the Greek, Hebrew, French, and German
books in Francis's library. He was reading Victor Cousin, S. T.
Coleridge, and Thomas Jouffroy. The German and French idealism which he read directly and the English version of it which
he saw in Coleridge's *Aids to Reflection* provoked him. He
would not accept the ideas of "those who questioned the inspiration of the Bible or the authenticity of miracles." Before
long, however, he would accept the European views he now
rejected and be among those he now criticized. But all of his
reading was not so serious, for, after reading some of Byron's
poetry, he wrote to Lydia that Byron was "a wicked poet, and
a wicked man." He was never able to separate a man from his
achievements; indeed, many years later, in 1858, in a series of
lectures on American statesmen, he insisted on judging the men
as well as their work. Parker was compelled to make moral
judgments.

While in Watertown, he began his first scholarly project. With
Francis's urging and help he began a criticism of the New
Testament: "It is, as you know, a subject on which the noblest
minds that philosophy has enlightened have been busy these
thousand years, and without exhausting the boundless subject."[5]
He never finished this particular project, though he worked on it
for years; but he later accomplished much the same thing with
the Old Testament. Another ambition formed during these years
was to become dean of the Divinity School, a position then
occupied by John G. Palfrey.

Nothing is too much for young ambition to hope, no eminence too
lofty for his vision, no obstacle too difficult for his exertions, and no
excellence unattainable. Patience, perseverance, prayer, have done something already; and when we consider that sincere desires are never
neglected, and real endeavors never unassisted, we need not despair of
making some approaches at least to the eminence Mr. Palfrey now
occupies. Would not this be truly delightful? No situation can be more

honorable, no task more pleasant, no prospect more celestial, than that of a virtuous, faithful clergyman.

But he was already forming ideas heretical to the Unitarian establishment which were to close that opportunity to him. Less than a month after he had expressed his ambition to succeed Palfrey, he remarked that the Psalms of David, if they are seen "as works of inspiration, they appear inconsistent with the character of God; but if we regard them as only the odes of a pious king, who yet had all the frailties of a man, they must be pronounced excellent, though often savoring of a revengeful spirit."[6] This approach was to be typical of much of his early theological scholarship: to look for the human surrounding the divine. Before entering the Divinity School, Parker had chosen both his vocation of ministry and scholarship. Friends in Watertown presented him with a loving cup when he left in 1834. It might later have reminded him that there he had discovered Lydia, Convers Francis, German scholarship, and Abolition—his whole life had been shaped by his two years in Watertown.

IV *Divinity School*

In April, 1834, Parker went to Cambridge to begin his studies in Harvard Divinity School. His second period of residence in the capital city of New England was far more successful than his first. Among his fellow students were several who were to become members of the Transcendentalist circle—John S. Dwight, Cyrus A. Bartol, Charles T. Brooks, Christopher Cranch—though none of them were ever among Parker's close friends. Curiously, the characteristic pattern of those students who achieved some measure of fame was to leave the ministry. Parker remained in a pulpit, yet he almost decided to leave the ministry—and he virtually left the Unitarian orbit to become one of its chief critics. But the aspect of his years in school most important for the future was neither his relations with fellow students nor those with the faculty which included Henry Ware, Jr.; Dean John G. Palfrey; or Andrews Norton, an outstanding scholar and a prominent opponent of the Transcendentalists.

These years marked the continuation of his efforts to become a first-rate scholar. He increased his study of languages, at least dabbling in Italian, Portuguese, Dutch, Icelandic, Chaldaic, Arabic, Persian, Coptic, Ethiopian, Russian, Swedish, and Danish.

Since classes occupied no more than half of any day, Parker could find time for all his work. As a fellow student, C. P. Cranch, recalled, "He made daily acquaintance with books which were sealed books to many old biblical scholars, and, to us youngsters of the school, were scarcely known even by name. He would dive into the college-library, and fish up huge, venerable tomes in Latin and Greek, and lug them up to his room, and go into them as a boarding-school girl would go into a novel." Their expectations were that he would be a scholar. They had other interests. Across the hall from Parker's room, No. 29, Cranch and John S. Dwight were singing or playing instruments one night. They slowly became aware of strange noises in the hall. When they opened the door, there was Parker, sawing on a log that was mounted on a horse. Cranch remembered that Parker "barely smiled" at their discovery of the little joke he had played to remind them of his presence.[7]

At the time he came to the Divinity School in 1834 he wrote of his beliefs to his nephew, Columbus Greene, a man of almost his own age: "I believe in the Bible." He continued, "I believe there is *one* God who has existed from all eternity, with whom the past, present, and future are alike present; that he is almighty, good, and merciful, will reward the good and punish the wicked, both in this life and the next. This punishment *may be* eternal; of course, I believe that neither the rewards nor punishments of a future state are corporal."[8] His beliefs were proper to a Unitarian, though his notion of all time as being conceived as present by God is one which had significant consequences for Parker and for other Transcendentalists as they considered human history. Parker's remarks on punishment reflect the doubts he was always to have. In the same letter he asserted that the books of the Bible were "written by men inspired by God, for certain purposes, but I do not think them inspired *at all times.*" This remark foreshadows his early work on the Bible, which began while he was still a student and which became his first substantial theological scholarship. Significant is his refusal to accept divine inspiration of the whole Bible.

In these letters Parker also gives his view of Christ: "Christ was the Son of God, conceived and born in a miraculous manner, that he came to preach a better religion by which man may be saved. This religion, as I think allows men the very highest happiness in this life, and promises eternal felicity in another world.

I do not think our sins will be forgiven because Christ died. I cannot conceive why they should be, although many good and great men have thought so. I believe GOD knows all that we shall do, but does not *cause* us to do anything." Parker carried his belief in free will before him always; to him, the achievements of men and nations resulted largely from the exercise of it; and the crucial burden for the condition of the world rested upon the individual. If sins could not be forgiven because of Christ's sacrifice, then the intermediary which most Christians recognized had been removed. By 1836 Parker was even ready to say, "I do not doubt that Jesus was a man 'sent from God' and endowed with power from on high; that he taught the truth and worked miracles; but that he was the subject of inspired prophecy I very much doubt."[9] Though Parker had not yet developed his final opinions on the divinity of Christ, he was moving rapidly away from the orthodox Unitarian position and toward his own radical views of Christ and miracles.

During Parker's years in the Divinity School he edited and contributed to the *Scriptural Interpreter,* which had been begun by Ezra Stiles Gannett in 1831. When Gannett became too ill to edit the publication, he passed it to Parker and two of his classmates, George M. Ellis and William Silsbee. By the end of the second year, when publication ceased, Parker was contributing more than both of the other editors. Gannett, intending the publication for the homes of Unitarian laymen, had not expected the pages of the *Scriptural Interpreter* to contain doctrines or ideas which went far beyond Unitarian orthodoxy; and he must have instructed the three Divinity School students to hew to this line. For the most part, they followed his wishes; but one day an anonymous letter addressed to the editors of the magazine arrived. The writer, "A Subscriber," attacked the young editors, and particularly Parker who had written the piece he mentions:

I read, in the last number of the *Scriptural Interpreter,* the article on the 52nd chapter of Isaiah, and with unmingled surprise and horror. What could possess you? What is the object of the theologians at Cambridge? Are they determined to break down the prophecies, and make our blessed Savior and his Apostles imposters and liars? Cannot our doctrines be sustained in any other way? Must the pious Christian be compelled to give up one passage after another, one book after another, one prophecy after another, until he has nothing left to stand upon but what is in common with the Deist? Where is it all to end? Tell us, I beseech you, that we may quit, if necessary, the ship before it is too late; before we have struck upon the last rock which the vessel of our faith will bear?[10]

Another paragraph in the same tone and with the same vagueness and alarm follows. The editors published a kindly note asking the subscriber to be specific so that his charges could be answered. Parker might have taken warning from this prophetic episode, but there is no indication his enthusiasm was affected.

Among the four hundred pages Parker published are his first studies in theology, in which he began his theological battles. His contributions to the *Scriptural Interpreter* include translations, commentaries, and such longer articles as the one on Job and another entitled "The Laws of Moses," which ran one hundred pages. One of his first contributions was "The Alleged Mistake of the Apostles" in which Parker sought to prove that they did not believe Christ would return during their lifetime, pointing out how destructive such teachings would have been as the years went on and Christ did not appear. To prove the book of Job was not written by Moses, Parker used literary analysis and showed it to be a poem containing "unnatural incidents" rather than a history. And again he commented on miracles: "A miracle is never wrought unless the occasion be adequate...." He soon had much more to say about miracles; in fact, the issue would become one identified with Parker and Parkerism. At the end of his article on Job, Parker confessed that many of his ideas and opinions "may be found in the commentaries of ancient and modern German writers."[11] In these two articles appear the methodology and approach that were to be Parker's, and especially prominent are rational and historical investigation.

Another revealing article is "How Ought the Bible To Be Read." Parker emphasized four necessities which he himself never neglected: (1) to read with reason, (2) with a consciousness of its antiquity, (3) with an awareness of the varying authors and, lastly, (4) with a feeling and sympathy for the nature of the work. This fourth necessity reveals the devotion which Parker always possessed and which his enemies always denied. The second and third reflect Parker's own predispositions to be continually aware of the historic aspects of the Bible which led him to question divine inspiration. But he is not yet ready to surrender belief in divine inspiration, as he reveals when he says of the laws of Moses; *"no man in the time of Moses could have devised such a code without miraculous aid.*"[12] But of the four rules for reading the Bible, the most important is the first. Parker believed one had to read with reason to decide upon the interpretation revealed; he would not accept a religion of faith and devotion without reason. This guide was to be his through the years of searching and interpreting the Scriptures, and he thought all men should use this tool.

V *Confidence and Doubt*

The work for the *Scriptural Interpreter* and his studies in the Divinity School prepared Parker for the first full-length scholarly project he would undertake, a translation of Wilhelm M. L. De Wette's *Einleitung in Das Alte Testament.* This work was begun during his candidating, the period during which the young graduate preached in churches seeking a permanent pastor. Parker preached in several small towns, including the fishing village of Barnstable, before accepting a place in West Roxbury at the Spring Street Church. Most of the time he was so far from Boston that he could not easily visit the city. When he missed one of Emerson's series of lectures, he wrote to Lydia: "You know I lamented the missing of Mr. Emerson's lectures, but a single walk along the banks of the Connecticut, or among the hills, or a moment's listening to the pine's soft music, have taught me more than Mr. Emerson and all the Boston Association of Ministers."[13] Although Parker thought nature to be the greatest teacher, he spent most of his life in his study in the city.

This apparent paradox might have plagued many of the Transcendentalists; even Thoreau, though he spent much of his time outdoors, was well read. But learning from nature meant more than contemplation while walking through woods; it also meant looking inward to one's own nature. The Transcendentalists search for knowledge led them to value both sensory and intuitive experience, as Parker's essay, "Transcendentalism," clearly establishes. Yet, the paradox cannot be entirely resolved. That scholars should value most highly non-literary experience may seem ironic, but in their view the reading was done to find support for opinions derived intuitively and to learn what other men said rather than to appreciate how they said it.[14]

Parker, like Emerson, wrote very little about the meaning and inspiration of the countryside, but he wrote a great deal about the nature of men. His whole scheme of thought is firmly anchored in his conception of the nature of man, his actual and potential state. For example, his proof of the existence of God and the necessity for religion rests on the nature of man in that man possesses a religious faculty. Much of Parker's theological scholarship is directed toward the end of showing the falsity of views that ignore the nature of man. But Parker's choice of vocation at the time he began his career in preaching was not this idealistic motivation of rectifying theology.

Facing the problems of his new vocation, he admitted his doubts about becoming a minister, confessing that he was responding to duty more than to his own desire:

One sole thing encourages me, to wit, I know that one who keeps God's "Laws of the Spirit of Life," and puts forth his might manfully in obedience thereto, be his might never so little—be it less than mine even—he has for his friend and ally and co-worker the entire almightiness and perfect virtue of God. With such a co-adjutor it is nobler to be conquered, dragged at the wheels of the enemy, yea, trodden to dust by his followers, who shout aloud, "Great is Mammon of the Yankees!" than to engage in any other warfare.

Therefore shall I go on; consequences I have nothing to do with, they belong to God—to me belongs only duty. All that I have I give

Seldom if ever again did Parker admit this motivation. Much of the rest of his life was spent in fidelity to duty at great cost. His personal vision sent him against Boston Unitarianism, against statutory law, and against the social and economic system. He remained a minister while others with beliefs similar to his left to fight on other grounds. Duty and obedience were the real and final keys to Parker's life, but the conflict between God's and man's laws brought him great pain.

A month before Parker's ordination on June 21, 1837, he had completed his translation of De Wette's work, though he added a great deal of commentary before sending it to a publisher. In April, he had married Lydia Cabot. The controversy which would soon involve him and become his first battleground had already begun. His friend George Ripley had written an article on James Martineau's *Rationale of Religious Inquiry* for the *Christian Examiner* in which he had challenged the Unitarian view of man and had raised the issues of miracles and the nature of man.

When Andrews Norton replied in the *Boston Daily Advertiser* from his orthodox Unitarian position, Parker, who was angry that Norton had deliberately attacked his friend, remarked: "The last time I saw Mr. R[ipley], I suggested that the first one who lifted a hand in this work would have to suffer; and I wished to push some old veteran German to the fore-front of the battle, who would not care for a few blows: but he thought there was no danger." [16] Parker eventually entered the battle under the pseudonym "Levi Blodgett" and confirmed that he was right and Ripley wrong: there was danger.

In 1836 Parker's friend and mentor, Convers Francis, expressed his estimate of the Unitarian situation: "I find the George Ripley is publishing *Discourses on the Philosophy of Religion;* besides, Brownson is out with his *New Views,* and Alcott with *Questions on the Gospels, for Children.* Then there is Furness' book, *Remarks on the Gospels,* so that it seems the spiritualists are taking the field in force. I have long seen that the Unitarians must break into two schools—the old one, or English school, belonging to the sensual and empiric philosophy, and the new one, or the German school (perhaps it may be called), belonging to the spiritual philosophy." [17]

Francis's pupil, Parker, was to become the pulpit leader of this new spiritual school. Though the fight would be a New England, almost a Boston, struggle, Theodore Parker acted in a manner similar to that of the Western pioneer: he used the tools provided by others,—Emerson, Ripley, and the Germans; and he did not enjoy the results of his labors in breaking the way. Only the generation after him, which included such men as O. B. Frothingham, would be able to work within a Unitarianism divorced from its Calvinistic heritage. Parker, in a rough and clumsy fashion, assaulted the walls of the Boston establishment and by his methods made enemies even of those who might have shared his views. His ambition and self-righteousness would not let him move slowly, tactfully, or respectfully. The country boy never differentiated the private study from the pulpit, the letter from the pamphlet, the home from the platform. He treated theology, history, society, and politics as battlegrounds on which he could win by speaking his mind without regard for his opponents' prejudices. Like his grandfather, he began the war others were to finish.

CHAPTER 2

The Young Clergyman

The first years in West Roxbury might have been those in which Parker carefully worked toward the goals he had set for himself. Apparently very much disappointed at not being offered a post at the Divinity School, he still might have become primarily a scholar, who did his parish work but more earnestly pursued his studies. In those New England days a Unitarian minister in good standing with the denominational leaders had little trouble publishing articles and books, but Theodore Parker would not and could not choose the respectable path of Boston Unitarianism. Other reform movements were to come later; but, in his first few years in West Roxbury, he became firmly identified with Transcendentalism and the new school in theology which Francis described.

Though Parker completed some important scholarship, he quickly demonstrated that he would not be satisfied to stand with Andrews Norton and other orthodox Unitarians. While he wrote a few pieces for the *Christian Examiner,* the leading Unitarian journal, he was also writing for Orestes Brownson's *Boston Quarterly Review* and for the Transcendentalists' *Dial.* He finished his translation of De Wette's *Introduction to the Old Testament* which was later published. Most important, he entered the fight between the two factions of Unitarianism under the name Levi Blodgett and, almost unwittingly, made his first mark in that fight with a single sermon, "A Discourse of the Transient and the Permanent in Christianity." Four years after his ordination, Parker's theological position was established but not through the careful scholarship or the original thinking that the young man had hoped would be his success.

I *Towards a Theological Position*

The task of establishing the specific and significant influences in the early years on a man who read as much as Theodore Parker is virtually impossible. However, a few important personal experiences which certainly helped shape his life and work can be specified. As has already been noted, Convers Francis introduced him to German theological scholarship and allowed Parker to use his library and thereby became an important influence. (That Parker felt hurt when Francis later seemed to reject him suggests how important the older man was.) Other important persons were those who belonged to two clubs which overlapped in membership: one was William Ellery Channing's group, sometimes called the "Friends," which included such Transcendentalists as A. Bronson Alcott and George Ripley; another was the Transcendentalist group itself which met as the "Symposium" or "Hedge's Club."

At the meetings of these groups Parker was able to participate in discussions of such topics as the progress of civilization, Emerson's lectures, and the personality of God. The members of these groups shared ideas and interests to such an extent that trying to point to individual influences is fruitless—nor is this book the place for a long discussion on the nature of Transcendentalism.[1] Brownson's opinion that they agreed primarily in their opposition to the old school remains an accurate statement of the common ground, and Parker soon became one of the chief spokesmen of this faction.

Before he became firmly identified as a member of the new movement, Parker was a contributor of seven reviews and seven articles to the respected *Christian Examiner*. The brief notices and reviews of dictionaries and lexicons were particularly appropriate for the young minister who had studied languages and who had ambitions of being a scholar. Among these articles which demonstrate his wide learning is his first, in March, 1838—a review essay of a three-volume history of Gnosticism in French by Jacques Matter with a review of earlier histories and a careful summary of the work. His second, less than a year later, is a similar work on Ackermann's *The Christian in Plato and in the Platonic Philosophy Developed and Presented,* in which Parker revealed his admiration for Plato.

A habit established in these early articles and one which Parker never entirely escaped is a restrictive fidelity to the authors whose works he reviews. So carefully did he summarize their work that his own ideas seldom emerged. Parker never became an original thinker but rather one who relied heavily upon the ideas and methods he had learned from others. His articles on Henry More and Ralph Cudworth show a brief interest in English thought which was to be almost entirely replaced by a fascination with German theologians. He most respected the importance of intuition in the thought of these Englishmen, and he later combined his own use of it with the historical method he had learned from the Germans. When he first noticed David Friedrich Strauss's *Life of Jesus,* he commented briefly on it saying little more than this: "no reliance [is] to be placed upon 'historical Christianity,' though the essential doctrine of the Christian religion [is] as true as ever."[2]

Additional study changed his mind about the importance of Strauss's work. In the July, 1840, issue of the *Christian Examiner* appeared his full review essay of the Strauss work. He calls it "the most remarkable work that has appeared in theology, for the last hundred and fifty years." Parker, who compares the German and English theologians of the past two centuries, concludes that Germany now produces the significant thinkers. The comment was an important one for his future among the Unitarians because such recognized scholars as Andrews Norton were denying the importance of the Germans. But Parker was not yet willing to stand up against Norton, whose *Evidence of the Genuineness of the Gospels* he here praises. Strauss, Parker charged, did not write in a religious spirit (a quality Parker always insisted upon); Strauss saw nothing but myths and did not believe in miracles.

At this point in his career, Parker himself felt "that the Bible, and in particular the New Testament, always rests on historical ground, though it is not common historical ground, *nor is it so rigidly historical that no legendary or mythical elements have entered it.*" Though Parker would not go so far as Strauss, he was clearly impressed by the place of historical truth. Parker thought Strauss's extreme view a necessary one if mankind is ever to come to believe "the only *essential* creed is the Christian motto, 'Be perfect, as your Father in Heaven is perfect,' and the only *essential* form of religion is Love to your neighbor as to yourself, and to God with the whole heart, mind, and soul."[3]

Within a year such statements were to make Parker infamous among the orthodox. Furthermore, he had stated a central aspect of his own creed which he never surrendered. The essay on Strauss contains the germs of the thought of the mature theologian soon to emerge.

II   *Divinity School Address*

While Parker was still contributing to the *Christian Examiner,* Emerson, who was to become the nominal leader of Transcendentalism, spoke at the home of Unitarianism. A significant statement of ideas shared to some extent by William Ellery Channing, Parker, and others is Emerson's *Divinity School Address* of the summer of 1838. Of this address, in which Emerson rejected the supernatural authority of the Scriptures, Parker wrote in his journal: "I shall give no abstract, so beautiful, so just, so true, and terribly sublime, was his picture of the faults of the Church in its present position. My soul is roused; and this week I shall write the long-meditated sermons on the state of the Church and the duties of these times." These subjects were to be his not for a week but, in large part, for the rest of his life.

With more reservations, he wrote to his friend George E. Ellis of Emerson's address, "It was the noblest of all his performances: a little exaggerated, with some philosophical untruths, it seems to me; but the noblest, the most inspiring strain I ever listened to. It caused a great outcry. . ."[4] Indeed, it did—for years. There were defenders, among them Parker himself who later made some of the central points his own; but most of the Unitarian clergy attacked Emerson and his address. Andrews Norton attacked not only Emerson and his work but also Victor Cousin, Thomas Carlyle, Friedrich Schleiermacher, P. B. Shelley, and everyone (and everything) he could identify with the new movement.

One part of the reaction was a discussion Parker heard at a meeting of the Boston Association of (Unitarian) Ministers on Emerson's Christianity, which was in doubt. Since no one denied Emerson was a "virtuous and a most devout man," the ministers had to admit that a man could be virtuous and not a Christian, or religious and yet an atheist, or neither religious nor virtuous. To Parker's delight, the clergymen could not resolve their dilemma. He thought he saw clearly the state of Boston Unitarianism: "It is quite evident there are now two parties among the Unitarians; one is for progress; the other says, 'Our strength is to stand still.' Dr. Channing is the real head of the first party: the other had no head. Some day or other there will be a rent in the party: not soon, I trust, however."[5] To a degree, Parker was to replace William Ellery Channing; Andrews Norton and especially N. L. Frothingham, the father of Parker's biographer, were to lead the conservatives.

Emerson maintained unobtrusive leadership of the Transcendentalists, and he remained aloof from many of the controversies of the day even when he would seem to be in the middle of them. As Oliver Wendell Holmes expresses it in his biography, Emerson was like Patroclus when the Greeks and Trojans fought over his body. Although Emerson was widely attacked for his address of 1838, it was George Ripley who became one of the first spokesmen for the Transcendentalists. He and Norton had clashed over Ripley's review of James Martineau's *Rationale of Religious Enquiry* in which he had attacked the Unitarian position on miracles, inspiration, and the relation between God and man; but his *Discourses on the Philosophy of Religion* and *Specimens of Foreign Standard Literature* had been accepted by the Unitarian press. The peace between Ripley and the conservatives was not to last.

The most well-known reply to Emerson's *Divinity School Address* is Norton's *Discourse on the Latest Form of Infidelity.* Asked to write it by the new "Association of the Alumni" of the Divinity School, he delivered his address on July 19, 1839, almost a year after Emerson had spoken. Actually, Norton's work was part of a continuing controversy in which he, Emerson, Ripley, and others, including Parker, eventually, engaged. Norton argued that those who deny miracles deny Christianity: "Nothing is left that can be called Christianity, if its miraculous character can be denied." Miracles furnish sensory evidence that man's reason can cope with: "There is . . . no mode of establishing religious belief, but by the exercise of reason, by investigation, by forming a probable judgment upon facts." Norton added that "the great majority of men" could not be expected to understand all the truths of Christianity; they had to rely upon "*belief on testimony,* the testimony of those who have examined a subject to their conviction of the truth of certain facts."[6]

The argument between Norton and the Transcendentalists involved two issues—miracles and reason. As Norton's statements suggest, he thought Christianity rested on the acceptance of biblical miracles as examples of supernatural intervention. Emerson, and later Parker, argued that miracles—unnatural events—could not happen because everything was ordered. They argued that Christianity rested on truths which every man could know to be true without physical demonstrations such as the phenomena Norton regarded as miracles. What Norton called reason, the Transcendentalists named Understanding; and for them, Reason was the name for intuition. (See footnote 14, Chapter 1, for further discussion of the distinction.) And while Norton argued that reason established the truth of religion, the Transcendentalists asserted that Reason (intuition) performed that function. While Norton doubted the capacity of most men to understand religious truths, the Transcendentalists believed that each man could—through Reason—understand them. Ripley, in his printed replies to Norton, challenged Norton's notion of an educated priesthood, "those who have examined a subject."

Ripley began the first of his three long replies with a tribute to the Divinity School and to the men it had sent forth who had discovered that their congregations needed new bases of faith. In the search to help their people, the ministers "had become convinced of the superiority of the testimony of the soul to the evidence of the external senses; the essential character of Christianity, as a principle of spiritual faith, of reliance on the Universal Father, and of the intrinsic quality and brotherhood of man, was made more prominent than the historical circumstances with which it was surrounded. . . ." Intuition and inspiration, therefore, were to the Transcendentalists more important than the authority of miracles described in the Bible.

Ripley accused Norton of declaring that those who did not agree with his doctrines were not Christians. Even Norton's title, *The Latest Form of Infidelity*, suggested this, since infidelity then meant the denial of the authority of Scripture. For Ripley, a belief in the authority of miracles was not the only "evidence of a divine revelation." He closed with an attack on a certain kind of scholar—Norton:

I honor the learned, when they devote their attainments to the service of society; when they cherish a stronger interest in the welfare of their brethren, than in the luxury of their books; when they bring the researches of science to the illustration of truth, the correction of abuses, and the aid of the sufferer; but if they do not acknowledge a higher light than that which comes from the printed page; if they confound the possession of erudition with the gift of wisdom; and above all, if they presume to interfere in the communion of the soul with God, and limit he universal bounty of Heaven within their "smoky cells," I can only utter my amazement.[7]

As the Transcendentalist scholars charged the orthodox Unitarian with submission to the printed page, they put themselves in a paradoxical position. Such dilemmas were in part responsible for Ripley's and many other Transcendentalist ministers' leaving the church; but Parker and others, especially some of his younger colleagues not yet active in 1839, tried to reform the Unitarian church.

In October, 1839, Parker gave his opinion of Ripley's reply to Norton to his friend William Silsbee, who had been one of the co-editors of the *Scriptural Interpreter:* he thought it "excellent, both in design and execution." Norton should be thankful "that he has fallen into the hands of a Christian man and not the clutches of a Philistine."[8] Parker, who knew both men well, had been following the controversy with care, keeping newspaper clippings in his journal. As early as the summer of 1838, when Emerson had given the address which started this stage of the battle between the new and the old factions of Unitarianism, Parker had clipped from the *Advertiser* the article, "The New School in Literature and Religion," which he had correctly ascribed to Norton. In this article Parker had read: "There is a general tendency among its [the new school's] disciples to disavow learning and reasoning as sources of their knowledge. The mind must be its own unassisted teacher."[9] Parker accepted the statement as truth, not as error. Though at least as late as January, 1839, he paid Norton a friendly visit, he could not stay out of the fight.

In 1840 Parker published *The Previous Question Between Mr. Andrews Norton and His Alumni Moved and Handled in a Letter to All Those Gentlemen* by Levi Blodgett. While Ripley had been enmeshed in three long letters in which he elaborately considered Norton's arguments, even those which were irrelevant, Parker tried to strike directly at the central issues. His assumption of the persona of a common man with no theological training is a rhetorical technique he was to try again, but he seldom managed it with skill. He began with the proposition that Christianity is based on essential truths innate in man, and he joined Ripley in arguing that miracles are not needed to prove the truths of Christianity. He emphasized that "religion must be made for man's nature" since it begins there. He believed Christ did perform miracles but that these prove no doctrine. Men believe the doctrines irrespective of the miracles.

Relying on his persona, Parker concluded "happily" that the "miracle-question is one of *theology,* and not of *religion.*"[10] But the persona of the raw Yankee is completely lost in the sophistication of most of the argument which contains clear statements of the Transcendentalists' anti-Lockean position. (The orthodox Unitarians based their arguments on the Lockean position that knowledge can be gained only through sense impressions.) The germs of much of Parker's later work are here—the denial of the authority of miracles, the separation of religion and theology, the emphasis on reason, the notion of a religious faculty in man, as well as other concepts. Parker was fortunate in entering the battle under a disguise immediately seen through and yet emerging without scars. Now, however, he was known and would be watched.

The conflict occurring among the Unitarians at this time resembled one which had taken place in a remarkably similar fashion only twenty years before. The Congregationalists wished to refuse the name Christian to the Unitarians; they charged infidelity; they argued that Unitarianism did not tend to form a better religious character; and they said the Unitarians were following German scholarship, German rationalism, German heresy.[11] Now the orthodox Unitarians were making the same charges against the members of the new movement, the Transcendentalists. So swiftly had one movement succeeded the other that some of the radicals in the first had become the conservatives of the second, and this situation increased the sharpness of the battles. The Unitarians, who held Boston and little more, were hardly secure in their doctrinal positions as the prophecies of the Congregationalists rang in their ears. The new movement seemed the fulfillment of the prophecies that Unitarian beliefs led to Deism and finally outside religion altogether.

One of the episodes in which Parker did not directly participate took place at the Berry Street Conference in 1840.[12] The question for discussion was, "Ought differences of opinion on the value and authority of miracles to exclude men from Christian fellowship and sympathy with one another." Parker attended but said nothing. He had, after all, recently made his opinions on this subject quite clear in the Levi Blodgett pamphlet; or he perhaps feared he would say too much. But in his journal he recorded his shock: "This is the 19th century! This is Boston! This among the Unitarians!" The conference itself concluded that differences in opinion should not disrupt fellowship though in fact they did. Parker resolved "in the coming year, to let out all the force of Transcendentalism that is in men. Come what will come, I will let off the Truth fast as it comes."[13]

This episode does not belong solely to the realm of biographical incident. Parker was to live by his declaration to "let off the Truth" whatever the consequences. He refused to be muzzled by the Berry Street Conference or by any other group of ministers. More than that, he was to pay little attention to the lessons he might have learned in watching the careful shaping of denominational opinion. In his righteousness he neglected entirely the necessity of defining a sect while the orthodox Unitarians were still struggling to give themselves an identity separate from the nineteenth-century Calvinists from whom they had so recently divorced themselves.

III   *Writing and Preaching*

Not realizing how committed he had become since leaving Harvard, Parker continued to plan as though he had not yet taken his first mature steps. In May, 1840, he recorded in his journal what he hoped to accomplish:

I must write an introduction to the New Testament—must show what Christianity is, its universal and its distinctive part. I must write a Philosophy of Man, and show the foundation of religion in him. In my days of leisure, when I am not hard at work—on a beautiful Sabbath, for instance, or in a moony night, or one filled with stars, when I walk out, this burden presses me heavily. I must do or die. I sit down to hard work, and then only do I feel free from this tormenting spirit; at other times I am consumed by self-reproach for the nothings I have accomplished, for the nothing I have undertaken. My heart beats audibly, so that my hand quivers. Hard work only relieves me for the time it lasts. But I must do much hard work before I can approach the *Introduction*. This I am now preparing for. Still harder work must be done before the *Philosophy* can come forth, and much more before the crown of *Theology* can be put on the work. Here is work for digging, for flying, and for resting, still yielding to the currents of universal being that set through a soul that is pure.[14]

In such quiet moments when he wrote in his journal, Parker looked away from the controversy with his elders in the Unitarian Church in Boston. He sought to direct his energies toward the great problems of philosophy and theology. But, whether he wished it or not, he was coming to a collision with the Unitarian establishment. He was by no means conscious of how challenging his published works were to them.

In June, 1840, Parker published in *The Dial* a reworking of his lecture "Inspiration"; and entitled it "The Divine Presence in Nature and in the Soul." A part of his answer to Norton, it continued Parker's elaboration on Emerson's remarks of 1838. For Parker, inspiration is the "direct and immediate action of God upon men." The *"mode"* of inspiration is "the felt and acknowledged presence of the Highest in the soul imparting this Truth," while the *"criteria"* is "the truth of the thought, feeling or doctrine." All men can be inspired, but they may differ in *"degree"* of inspiration." Parker describes the omnipresence of God which is central to this intuitive process metaphorically: "The fullness of the divine energy flows inexhaustibly into the crystal of the rock, the juices of the plant, the splendor of the stars, the life of the Bee and Behemoth."

This passage contains the heart of Parker's belief in the presence of God and in the relation between God and man. The relation permits the possibility of future Christs—that God will "create a soul yet larger and nobler than Jesus" who will lead the way to "a more perfect religion." It also gives a more immediate possibility: "Now, as in the day of Moses, or Jesus, he who is faithful to Reason, and Conscience, Affection and Faith, will, through these receive an inspiration to guide him all his journey through."[15]

These doctrines open to every man possibilities which Norton and other orthodox Unitarians could not accept; and by November, 1840, Parker found that few men would exchange pulpits with him: "I should laugh outright to catch myself weeping because the Boston clergy would not exchange with me!"[16] But, in fact, he was to weep. The skirmish which Emerson began in 1838 had by 1840 fallen heaviest on Theodore Parker, and much more was yet to come.

Though Parker took advantage of various opportunities to

learn about the reform movements of his day, he did little in these early years outside his work in theology. He attended the Non-resistant Convention (but recorded in his journal that he did not believe in passive resistance) and the meeting of the Friends of Universal Reform known as the Chardon Street Convention. He regretted having been one of those who called the Chardon Street Convention at which the reform of the church, the ministry, and the Sabbath were discussed because even his friends chided him for becoming identified with the radicalism of the meeting. His regret in response to the criticism suggests that he was not prepared to be an active radical at the time. He still preferred his little Spring Street Church which allowed him to preach as he wished and to devote a minimal amount of time to work among the congregation. Even when offered a church in Lexington, Massachusetts, he turned it down as disadvantageous. He had resolved "to do more through the *Press* than the *Pulpit*," though the resolution was as much forced upon him as chosen.[17] To have decided at this time to work exclusively through the pulpit would at best have been innocent since no eminent pulpit position was open to him.

Parker's early life of economic poverty and intellectual richness led to great ambition, but he lacked clear objectives and he always doubted his abilities and his achievements. Every publication brought less success than he had expected. Though the lack of children was the only outward sign of failure in his marriage that he admitted, he occasionally hinted at other disappointments there. As early as the winter of 1837 he mentioned the loss of hope which he could find no longer on earth but specified no cause.[18] Since that year marked his marriage and his settling in his first permanent church, the loss of hope was presumably related to one or the other of those events. The causes of his depression were his failures to achieve his ambitions as scholar, minister, father, and self. In none did he achieve the perfection or fulfillment he believed could be his.

This sense of frustration, coupled with his belief in the possibility of perfection, encouraged him in his encounters with the Unitarian establishment, the social and economic systems, and the institution of slavery. It also drove him from one field of endeavor to another though without the frenetic movement of Orestes Brownson. While Parker later saw a logic and unity to his life's work in religion, social reform, and antislavery, the slow but continual change of emphasis indicates his search for less frustrating and more rewarding areas. The insight into the unity of his work was yet distant as Parker clung to his first ambition of becoming a renowned theologian and worked at developing his ideas in articles and sermons.

IV *Early Sermons*

Not many could have been acquainted with the early sermons of the young minister since few were published until later. In those now available there are a few signs of the direction in which he was moving. For example, in "Spiritual Indifference," a sermon of 1837, his first year of preaching, he speaks of the changes which have taken place in Christianity, urging that it is not an empty form. Looking back on his statement, one can conclude he was working toward a conception of the permanent in Christianity.

The very title of another sermon, "The World Belongs to Each Man," suggests his Transcendentalist view of the individual and the importance he later gave to the intuitive truths available to the individual. Parker's later doctrines also appear in "The Application of Religion to Life," for one of his greatest efforts was to make that application. In this sermon he made one of his earliest statements of the function of government, to prevent crime and to prevent poverty; he never departed from this view. Neither did he give up another view stated here—that the earthly object of religion is to make this world a better place. His notion of salvation was, therefore, primarily temporal rather than eternal; one seeks the perfect life here rather than in the here-after.[19] Already, then, he was concentrating on the place of religion in life, on the permanent in Christianity, and on the function of the individual in reforming society.

As Parker continued to work on the theological system he someday hoped to complete, he speculated about these matters in his journal while presenting the same ideas as established truth in his sermons. In the spring of 1841 he confessed in his journal that he did "not know what to make of" miracles, but those which "contradict the natural law—such as the transub-stantiation of bread, water, &c., the sending the devil into the swine, the resurrection of dead men, the resurrection of Jesus himself—all these have nothing to do with Christianity."[20] He was searching for the bedrock of Christianity, for the permanent rather than for the transient; and he realized that the Christianity of the nineteenth century would at some time seem as strange as that of the ninth appeared a millennium later. And Parker wondered if his own interpretations might not finally seem as wrong as those that had preceded them. Other Unitarians asked such questions only in their studies; Parker often presented his answers in public.

V *Fame and Notoriety*

About the time Parker was questioning the truth and meaning of miracles in his journal, he preached at the ordination of Charles G. Shackford at the South Boston Unitarian Church; the Unitarian world shook in response to Parker's "A Discourse of the Transient and Permanent in Christianity." Yet, as Chadwick suggests, "It is difficult to reconstruct the Unitarian mind that was so shocked and terrified by this enthusiastic affirmation of the permanence of essential Christianity and the greatness of the spiritual in man."[21] After all, the sermon was not original; at the installation of Orestes Brownson in 1834, George Ripley had first preached his sermon "Jesus Christ, the Same Yesterday, Today, and Forever" in which he had said: "With a strong desire for the unchangeable and everlasting the human soul is placed in the midst of perishable and transitory things."

For Ripley, "The Immutability of our Saviour consists in the Immutability of the religious truths which he taught," rather than because *He* taught them. Those truths which are not perishable and transitory are "the essential principles of Truth to which Christ bore witness as the Messenger of God."[22] These notions Parker repeated, and he knew that the sermon was not his best work. Since he recognized that he was in part restating his friend Ripley's ideas, he showed the sermon to him and he agreed that it was weak and repetitive. But it was not to the quality of the sermon that the clergy responded.

Parker began, as he often did, with Christ and His words, emphasizing the permanence of these and the changes in Christianity. "While true religion is always the same thing," he told this audience containing many fellow clergymen. "what men call Christianity" is continually changing. Christianity is the transient; "the eternal truth of God" is the permanent. Emphasizing the importance of the permanent, Parker said little about what men should do with the transient. He referred again and again to the historical changes of interpretation that he knew so well from his then current work on De Wette's *Introduction to the Old Testament*. He did not neglect the problem of the inspiration of the authors, because, though he had already published an article on it in *The Dial,* it still troubled him. Yet he also spoke with eloquence of the blessings of the Bible:

> You trace its path across the world from the day of Pentecost to this day. As a river springs up in the heart of a sandy continent, having its father in the skies, and its birth-place in distant unknown mountains; as the stream rolls on, enlarging itself, making in that arid waste a belt of verdure wherever it turns its way; creating palm groves and fertile plains, where the smoke of the cottager curls up at eventide, and marble cities send the gleam of their splendor far into the sky,—such has been the course of the Bible on the earth. . . . There is not a boy on all the hills of New England; not a girl born in the filthiest cellar which disgraces a capitol in Europe, and cries to God against the barbarism of modern civilization; not a boy nor a girl all Christendom through, but their lot is made better by that great book.

But the truth of Christ's words rest not on His testimony any more than the truths of science rest on the authority of their discoverers. The truth is not dependent on testimony or authority; "Christianity . . . is true, like the axioms of geometry, because it is true, and is to be tried by the oracle God places in the breast." The permanent in Christianity "is absolute, pure morality; absolute, pure religion." It contains one creed: "there is a God." These truths are discovered by those "things highest in man's nature"— "reason, conscience, and faith."[23] Near the end he warned that, if one relied solely on the current notions of Christianity rather than on its permanent truths, he must necessarily have his faith shaken by every contradiction he finds in the Bible and in history. The shaking of his own faith led Parker in his search for a more permanent religion.

The remarkable reaction to the sermon was not immediate, but from the later uproar one might suppose men ran screaming from the church. The first response came from orthodox ministers who had attended the ordination services. One demanded Parker's arrest for blasphemy, and before long, the Unitarian clergy joined in the outcry. Parker could not be removed from his church unless his own congregation wished to dismiss him, and it had repeatedly heard the ideas expressed in the South Boston sermon.

The newspapers were full of comments on the sermon and its author. A Unitarian layman wrote to the Boston *Courier:* "I would rather see every Unitarian congregation in our land dissolved and every one of our churches occupied by other denominations or razed to the ground than to assist in placing a man entertaining the sentiments of Theodore Parker in one of our pulpits."[24] Parker was labeled an infidel and a blasphemer, and he was associated with Thomas Paine and Voltaire. (Ironically, Parker later declined an invitation to speak on the anniversary of Paine's birth on the ground that he had "not the smallest sympathy" with Paine's view of religion.[25])

For Parker, an immediate effect of the sermon was the cancellation of exchanges of pulpits which had been arranged by Parker with his fellow clergymen. By July, a few months after the sermon, he could count on at most twelve of his brethren to exchange pulpits with him. Congregations were asking their ministers and prospective ministers if they would exchange with Parker; ministers, to test their own positions, asked themselves if they would exchange with him. Parker had achieved a notoriety he would never escape.

Parker, and his early biographers, found it difficult to understand the strength of the reaction to the sermon, because they neglected its relation to the earlier Congregationalist-Unitarian controversy and to its non-doctrinal aspects. (See pp. 33-38 above.) From the point of view of the clergy, the sermon was an attack upon the institution of the church. When Parker attacked what he called "the transient in Christianity", he was speaking about every aspect of contemporary churches. The sermon could easily be taken as an attack upon the clergymen, for he had in effect said to his fellow ministers, "What you are doing and most of what you are preaching is the part of Christianity that is temporary; in fact, most of what you are doing is scarcely needed, since it will pass away as another generation takes our place." The Unitarian establishment was too young to absorb such criticism; and, doctrinal matters aside, the leaders of the sect could not permit such attacks on their institution.

Parker did not expect such reactions because he had heard rumors of Emerson's acceptance among the clergy and because he knew others shared his own opinions. Some of the younger clergy, particularly, were moving in this direction. Furthermore, he knew that some of the Unitarians were talking privately at least in new ways about miracles; that "many half entertained [the ideas he expressed]; more were dallying with them in an amateur way; a few held them in their studies as literary speculations, but breathed no whisper of them out of doors."[26] They might have ignored Parker, but they were too uncertain of the ideas, too afraid of the effect on laymen, too fearful of the comments by the Congregationalists, and too insecure in their recently established sect.

John Weiss, a Unitarian minister and Parker's first biographer, thought the sermon brought to the foreground once more the question of the supernatural quality of Christ, a question which the Unitarians could not dispense with, because it formed a doctrinal basis for the Unitarian movement. The Unitarians' view of the question was summarized by Weiss: "If Christ is inspired by means of a law which makes the same inspiration possible to all men, the supernatural distinction of his nature is no longer credible. The denial of miracles and of every exclusive element of divinity, is only a question of time and boldness." Parker proposed to take away Christ's divinity.

At this time, wrote Weiss, "the Unitarians venerated Christ as a teacher, having discarded him as a person of the Trinity and a sacrificial agent." But "To construct an adequate idea of such a person, through whom men are to be saved by the more rational process of believing his remedial truth, it was necessary to secure the conditions of infallibility and authority for the truth, which is to save. The infallibility was provided in special inspiration, the authority was claimed under the miraculous attesting acts."[27] Though not part of the Trinity, Christ was an infallible teacher who performed authoritative miracles. Parker was anticipating a change in Unitarian doctrine which many of the clergy were not yet ready to accept.

Parker later recalled that he worried "the sermon would be reckoned tame and spiritless, for it so poorly and coldly expressed what burned in my heart like a volcano." He simply "wished to show that religion was independent of the foolish doctrines men have piled upon it. I wanted to break the yoke of bondage bound on men's necks, and have done what I could to make men better here and hereafter." Always, he was slow to realize what men would accept; therefore, partly out of innocence but largely out of tenacity, Parker continued on the path of publishing the truth as he found it.

In June, only two months after the notorious South Boston sermon, Parker rejected an invitation to give a series of lectures in the Masonic Temple in Boston during the following winter on his view of the Christian life. "I know of no finite happiness so great as that which attends a successful attempt to set forth the great truths of religion, on which our welfare depends," wrote Parker in his rejection as he gave as his only substantial reason a plea that he did not think he could do what they asked.[28] Later he accepted this offer and gave the lectures to large crowds. In the spring of 1842 he published them as *A Discourse of Matters Pertaining to Religion.* During this period he also was publishing in *The Dial* and completing his work on De Wette. Each of these efforts increased the opposition to him and to his work.

CHAPTER 3

The Theologian

Parker's last three years in West Roxbury were marked by his contributions to *The Dial*, the publication of the *Discourse*, the translation of De Wette's work, and his first trip to Europe. Most of his published work brought him more notoriety among the orthodox. The very work which led to his invitation to preach in Boston was that which provoked the attempt to force him out of the Boston Association of Ministers. No doubt Parker was encouraged by his success among the laity and by a small number of ministers to continue his attacks on the Boston Unitarian establishment and its theology. Though the neo-calvinist orthodox theology was included in Parker's targets, representatives of that school rarely attacked him with such ferocity as the Unitarians. To the orthodox, Parker was an outsider. Many of them would not even see *The Dial*, the periodical to which Parker contributed his early radical articles.

I *The Dial*

The Dial, the chief literary organ of Transcendentalism, was projected as early as 1835 but it did not actually appear until four years later. At a meeting of the Symposium at Cyrus A. Bartol's house on September 18, 1839, Bronson Alcott suggested the name of the publication as it began over the objections of Orestes Brownson who wanted his *Boston Quarterly Review* to be the published voice of the movement. *The Dial* was intended to be an original journal, not controlled by a group such as the Democrats (Brownson's quarterly) or by the Unitarians (*Christian Examiner*). Margaret Fuller was the editor for the first two years; George Ripley helped, but he soon became too involved in Brook Farm to do much work. To list the contributors over the four years of its life would be to list the Transcendentalists.

Parker, who was present at the inception of *The Dial* in 1839, contributed a number of articles; but he had no control over the publication. Though Parker's articles sold some issues, he was close neither to Emerson nor to Margaret Fuller, who once said of Parker, "He cannot be the leader of my journal. . . ." She did, however, respect his writing and his learning; and she even expected Parker or Emerson to assume direction of the journal. In March, 1842, Emerson did become the editor. Parker would have changed the course of the magazine perceptively, since he disliked the contributions of Thoreau and Alcott and probably some of the others which gave *The Dial* its rather ethereal aspect.[2] After Emerson took charge, Parker's contributions became less frequent, but his trip to Europe rather than some disagreement between him and Emerson was probably the cause.

Parker contributed to *The Dial* ten substantial pieces which form a map of his interests and ideas in this period of his early maturity. Like his first article, "The Divine Presence in Nature and in the Soul," the second, "A Lesson for the Day: or The Christianity of Christ, of the Church, and of Society," brought animosity from the orthodox Unitarians. Some of the ideas which he would later present in his South Boston sermon are in the latter article which appeared in the October, 1840, issue of *The Dial.* He described the various forms of Christianity, beginning with the true Christianity of the early period, its perfection in the Christianity of Christ, its adulterated form in the contemporary churches, and the popular view of it that is scarcely related to the perfect view. There are at least suggestions of a denial of the divinity of Christ, of the supernatural authority of miracles, and of validity of the Scriptures. Though his attacks could be applied to the non-Unitarian orthodox, the leaders of his own sect could, and soon did, see themselves as the target. The article in *The Dial,* however, could be ignored as the public statement in a Unitarian Church a few months later could not.

Some months after the South Boston sermon, Parker attacked in the issue for July, 1841, the more influential groups. In "The Pharisees," he wrote of the "moral monsters" who have always existed. He described them in biblical times but quickly moved to the contemporary scene to speak of the pharisees of the fireside, the press, the street, politics, the church, and the pulpit. Taking each in turn, in an ascending order, Parker employed barbed sarcasm, and the pharisees he described were his targets for the rest of his life. He found few pharisees of the fireside since few are hypocrites in their own homes. The pharisee of the press is one who is always on the "right" side; that of the street is a kind of confidence man "who cheats you in the name of honor"; that of politics claims honesty but is "all things to all men," capable of being both for and against slavery. The pharisee of the church is the layman who goes to church on Sunday and sends "Bibles to the Heathen on the deck of his ship, and rum, gunpowder, and cast-iron muskets in the hold. The aim of this man is to get the most out of his fellow-mortals, and to do the least for them, at the same time keeping up the phenomena of Goodness and Religion."

But Parker reserved his sharpest attack for the pharisee of the pulpit. Form rather than substance is what this pharisee practices, since he believes in the authority of church and minister. Among these pharisees are those who do not think, but more dangerous are those who do because they "think one thing in their study, and preach a very different thing in their pulpit." "In his study, the Testament is a collection of legendary tales; in the pulpit it is the everlasting Gospel. . . ."[3] The reaction to his South Boston sermon taught Parker that what men said in their studies was not necessarily what they said from their pulpits, in the newspapers, or at the meetings of the Boston Association.

But Parker's articles are not only attacks on his brethren. In "Primitive Christianity," for example, he asserted that, during the time of Christ, Christianity had only four maxims: "Love man," "Love God," "we that are strong ought to bear the burdens of the weak," and "we must give good for evil." It is to this that Parker urged a return. In "Thoughts on Theology" he called for a science of theology such as that practiced in Germany—study "in a philosophical spirit, and the method of a science." He asked what the work of Michael Faraday and William Herschel would have been if they had used the prevalent theological method in their science, and he ridiculed the procedure of searching for truth while adhering to a belief which rejects all that does not conform to that belief. He called for the scientific and historical approach which he tried to use in his own work.[4] Parker's articles are often marked by such a combination of criticism and advocacy, but his technique of persuasion through attack angered members of the Unitarian establishment and provoked men to accuse Parker of negativism and of destroying old without substituting new ideas. To a degree this change is true, but Parker himself was always convinced he was supplying viable alternatives to the beliefs and methods he rejected.

In this early period, Parker could still inject humor into his articles. He began "German Literature" with a satiric sketch of the German influence in the United States, its perniciousness, its corruption of youth, its immorality: "It has often been a matter of astonishment to us, that the guardians of the public welfare did not discover German literature when it first set foot in America, and thrust it back into the ocean; and we can only account for the fact of its extension here, from the greater activity of Evil in general."[5] After several pages of such play, directed at Norton and other conservatives, Parker gave German literature the highest praise.[6]

Another secular piece, "Thoughts on Labor," is a laudation of labor which contains some of Parker's most banal writing: "Manual labor is a blessing and a dignity." He also voices some of the ideals of the utopian communities—that, in a "rational" society, labor and culture would be balanced; that manual labor alone is ruinous of other capacities; that society should permit every man such perfection as he can achieve. In many articles written for *The Dial,* and particularly in this, Parker began to show a concern for economic issues: "Thus, by the treachery of one part of society, in avoiding their share of the work; by their tyranny in increasing the burden of the world; an evil is produced quite unknown in a simpler state of life, and a man of but common capacities not born to wealth, in order to insure a subsistence for himself and his family, must work with his hands so large a part of his time, that nothing is left for intellectual, moral, aesthetic, and religious improvement."

Poverty so rules such a man that he can scarcely read his Bible or pray. "There must," wrote Parker, "be a great sin somewhere in that state of society, which allows one man to waste day and night in sluggishness or riot, consuming the bread of whole families, while from others, equally well-gifted and faithful, it demands twelve, or sixteen, or even eighteen hours of hard work of the twenty-four, and then leaves the man so weary and worn, that he is capable of nothing but sleep,—sleep that is broken by no dream!"[7] The system must be altered; men must have time for improvement and enjoyment. Of the three ways of getting wealth—robbery, trade (which is like robbery except that cunning is used in place of force, and gold in place of the sword), and production—only the last, in which an increase of value is infused by mental or physical labor, is legitimate.

To illustrate the nature of the contemporary social-economic order, Parker wrote a fable of the village of Humdrum. After machines are invented, people need to work fewer hours; but the leaders, the longest heads in Humdrum, decide that free time is dangerous and again set the people to working fourteen hours a day. The surplus of over production is exported, and luxuries imported. The "strong-headed men grow rich," while the others work more than before and are blessed with ribbons and gloves— the only evidence that the people are better off since they still have no time to develop their minds. Crimes increase, bringing courts, lawyers, judges, jails, and jailers. This is the history of the nations Parker knows.

But education, "Christian labor," and "Christian wealth" can provide the solution.[8] Though Brook Farm and many other utopian communities were functioning at this time, Parker did not refer to any of them as a model for the ideal society. Though Parker can with justification be characterized as a utopian, he always worked from the existing situation to the ideal. To withdraw from society or to begin anew were not congenial to this New Englander who insisted upon facts, be they statistical, historical, or theological.

II *Brook Farm*

Brook Farm is another venture associated with the Transcendentalists. Though *The Dial* clearly belongs to the movement, the experimental community had a more tenuous connection with it. None of the leaders—Emerson, Alcott, Hedge, Parker—lived there; in fact, Parker was related to the Brook Farm experiment primarily through his friendship with its leader, George Ripley. Parker's church at West Roxbury was less than three miles from the community, and many of its inhabitants came on Sundays to hear his sermons. Parker was a constant visitor to Brook Farm and did at one time consider moving there, though not out of faith in the project. Moreover, his trip to Europe in 1843 and his assumption of the responsibilities of a Boston congregation in 1845 helped to keep him from Brook Farm. And Parker also knew something of farming, especially of farming that did not pay and of farming on land that was not one's own. He must have remembered how he had had to steal hours from the land in order to pursue his reading.

But if the agricultural work at Brook Farm did not appeal to him, much less did other aspects. Since Parker's ambition was personal and substantial, he saw that to join the idealists at Brook Farm would have interfered with his ambitions for the sake of an experiment he could not value highly. When he rejected the opportunity to move to a Lexington church, he reasoned that he could spend more time in his study if he stayed in West Roxbury. He needed privacy, solitude, and time for his own work in these days when his scholarly ambition was still foremost. Any impulse to join the community would have been based on his desire to escape the battles with the Unitarian clergy rather than agreement with the ideals of Ripley. Had he joined, he, like Hawthorne, would soon have left.

Parker's brief inclination to leave the ministry came in part as a result of the book which was the product of his first series of lectures in Boston. Where he received the last proof of *A Discourse of Religion* in May, 1842, he realized there would be objections to the work. This realization continued to be on his mind as he wrote a month later to Convers Francis urging him to accept a position at the Harvard Divinity School. Parker complained, though denying he was doing so, that he had "no fellowship from the other clergy." No one who attended his ordination would have anything to do with him; only one or two members of the Boston Ministerial Association and only a few outside it would exchange pulpits with him. He speculated on writing one hundred and four sermons a year for the one hundred and four people who attended his church. If he stayed in West Roxbury, no one would hear him. He stated unequivocally his reaction to the prospect of staying in West Roxbury: *"Now this I will not do."*

In this letter Parker indicated that he might go to Brook Farm. He was so depressed and enraged that he thought of going there or of leaving his pulpit to study seven or eight months of the year and to preach or lecture the rest of the time. In a letter to Francis written a few months earlier, Parker had claimed he had "never cared much for the sympathy of other men, and never less than now; but once in a great while I feel it is not altogether pleasant to stand alone, to be viewed with suspicion and hatred." Francis had warned him that "he that defies public opinion is like the man who spits in the wind; he spits in his own face."[9] Yet Parker was surprised and disappointed that some clergymen he does not name whom he had expected to stand with him had turned their backs. Despite feelings of disappointment, depression and rejection, and the likelihood that the book would cause him further trouble—as these letters to Francis reveal that it did—Parker had published *A Discourse of Religion.*

III   *A Discourse of Religion*

In his Preface, Parker wrote that the book is an expanded version of the lectures he had given the winter before in Boston. He presented his ideas first as lectures because of "the state of theological learning amongst us," presumably meaning that he found a platform when he could not find a publisher. His subject is that of the South Boston sermon more completely and carefully worked out to reveal the "true views of God, man, the relation between them, and the duties which come of that relation." In the Introduction which follows the Preface he repeated his intention "to recall men from the transient Form to the eternal Substance" and complained particularly of the divorce of religion from life.

These themes are to be Parker's great ones. He had chosen religion as his vocation; he had chosen not only the ministry of the pulpit, the funerals, the marriages, and the visiting of the sick, but also scholarship and the application of his religious ideas. Attacking the separation of religion and life, Parker in this book struck at the "popular theology"—orthodoxy—with its view of man as "a spurious issue of the devil" who "deserves nothing but damnation." It is appropriate to examine this work in some detail because Parker seldom went far beyond the ideas, method, and approach of this first major work.

In his first lecture Parker argues the central preposition of the series: the principle that religion proceeds from the spiritual wants and needs of man, from his soul which is the religious faculty. Without this principle, there is a phenomenon without a cause. The religious element is part of man's nature as are the body, the understanding, the affections, and the moral sense; but it is deeper than these. Just as the faculty of sight implies objects to be seen, so the religious faculty implies an object: "natural want . . . implies satisfaction." God's existence is established through an "intuition of REASON," or, as the orthodox theologians de-

scribe it, "REVELATION FROM GOD." Therefore, no pretense of proving
the existence of God can be made.

Given God and the religious faculty in man, religion itself can
be defined as "VOLUNTARY OBEDIENCE TO THE LAW OF GOD INWARD
AND OUTWARD OBEDIENCE." Theology is man's thoughts about
religion, and to explain this distinction Parker relies on an analogy.
As the stars are the subject of astronomy, so religion is the subject
of theology. Having defined his subject, Parker begins to describe
its history. He identifies the stages of religion—fetishism, polytheism and monotheism—and finds they correspond to the stages
of civilization. Slavery belongs to the religion, and concomitant
society, of polytheism. In the present state of monotheism, there
is one God and no place for war and slavery, "no envy, strife,
or confusion in the divine consciousness, to justify hostility among
men." For Parker, progress has lead to the present state which
is more perfect and more easily perfectible than previous states.
Religious history "is a series of developments, all tending towards
one great and beautiful end, the harmonious perfection of Man."
So firmly does he believe in progress that he proclaims, "The
Kingdom of Heaven is not behind but before us."[10] For such a state,
Parker works and educates mankind.

In his second lecture (Book II of *A Discourse*), Parker deals
with inspiration, a subject which had provoked continual quarrels
with his opponents. Here he voices the view which led to a charge
of pantheism against him and other Transcendentalists. For Parker,
"All Nature . . . is but an exhibition of God to the senses. . . ."
Although Parker does not put God into nature, confusion can
arise when he concludes that "He must be infinitely present in each
point of space. This immanence of God in Matter [and in man] is the
basis of his influence. . . ."

To elucidate this relationship of God and matter, Parker sets
forth a three-part division of religion into naturalism, supernaturalism, and spiritualism. Naturalism, the doctrine most widely
held in New England, denies the immanence of God in man and
in matter and shares with supernaturalism the belief that there is
nothing in man "which was not first in the senses; whatever
transcends the senses can come to him only by a Miracle."[11]
Parker opposes this Lockean view of orthodoxy and puts himself
among those who hold the "natural-religious view, or spiritualism"
which places God in man and permits inspiration. He thereby
denies the philosophical and religious bases of orthodoxy.

Having grappled with the fundamental elements of religion and its philosophical basis, Parker moves to the particular elements of Christianity—Christ, the Bible, and the church. Christ, whom the Unitarians value virtually as much as the other Protestant sects, Parker denies as a teacher of Christianity. Rather, Christ taught a "form of Religion,—Piety and Morality." Parker denies the divinity of Christ; his authority; and the truth, force, and importance of miracles. In Book IV of *A Discourse,* he generously estimates the force and meaning of the Bible for men; but he concludes that "the Bible is a human work, as much as the *Principia* of Newton or Descartes, or the Vedas and Koran."[12] He discusses its historical errors, its prophetic problems, and its parallels with other sacred books including parables whose analogues are found in other religions.

In Book V Parker defines the church as the men and women who make up that body which worships as Christian. While denying any real and lasting substance to the church, he tries to prove it has significance and an important task even as he undermines many of its traditional functions. Religion can do what science cannot; for example, it can hold a village together. But the church only has a significance for a particular time and place. Protestantism is not his religion as it includes the belief that "the canonical Scriptures of the Old and New Testaments are the direct word of God, and therefore the only Infallible Rule of religious Faith and Practice." While Protestantism, gives the individual freedom of interpretation, it also permits him to find religious truth only in the Scriptures—a restriction which Parker could not accept. As he moves toward the conclusion of the work, he dismisses sin as "a point which mistaken men pass through in their development" and atonement (vicarious sacrifice) which he calls a "theological fiction" because "no man can be a substitute for another, for sin is infinite and he finite."[13]

These doctrines of sin and atonement which Parker attacks belonged to one of his targets in the book, the "Popular Theology" which is the theology of the major Protestant sects. (In a sermon Parker had said, "The common theology made God a King, not a Father; Christ the Master, not the brother of us all; and man a worm, a child of God's wrath, not the Son of his Love, made in the Father's image."[14] He thought of himself as continuing the revolution began by William Ellery Channing against the common theology.)

Against the "Popular Theology" he opposes a set of doctrines which starts from the concept of God as Father "infinite in power, wisdom, and love." The keynote is goodness, not sin:

It denies original sin, or admitting that, makes it of no effect, for Christ has restored all to their first estate. . . .

Its Hell is not eternal, for the Infinite Love of God must make the whole of existence a blessing to each man.

This system allows no ultimate evil, as a background of God; believes in no vindictive punishment.

Each man must be his own Christ, or he is no Christian

Parker admits that no sect is based on this system, though the Unitarians and Universalists come closest. He pleads for the Unitarians to adopt it and to teach "that man is greater than the Bible, ministry or church, that God is still immanent in mankind, that man saves himself by his own and not another's character, that a perfect manly life is the true service, and the only service God requires, the only source of well-being now or ever. . . ."[15] If Unitarianism does not accept these beliefs, it must surrender its lead to others. This set of doctrines which Parker proposed for the Unitarians is essentially the religion he preached for the rest of his life and the religion he himself attempted to practice.

IV   *Other Clashes with the Unitarians*

The Unitarians whom Parker usually included in the orthodox Christianity that he attacked could not ignore the revolutionary criticism from one of their own clergymen. They rejected his theology, and he thought they had rejected him. He would not leave the denomination, and they would not disown him. In the fall and winter of 1841, as the response to his work continued, he even gave another series of lectures in Boston. This series of invitational lectures he called "Six Plain Sermons for the Times." Meanwhile, the reaction to the first series became a continuation of that to the South Boston sermon and to the articles in *The Dial;* but there was some praise. Englishmen, particularly James Martineau, were impressed. Orestes Brownson devoted a whole issue of the *Boston Quarterly Review* to it, describing Parker's main purpose as an attempt to dispose of supernaturalism.[16] But the editor of the *Christian Examiner* cut out the few words of praise the reviewer had included. Convers Francis would not allow *A Discourse of Religion* to be dedicated to him. While the reaction continued, the October issue of *The Dial* was published. It included an article by Parker on the Hollis Street Council.

The Hollis Street Council had met in 1841 to discuss the position of Reverend John Pierpont and his congregation. Pierpont had preached against slavery, intemperance, and other sins committed by members of his congregation in their occupations and in their private lives; subsequently, they had asked for an investigation which was made by the Council. In his article, Parker wrote of the duty of the minister to be concerned with truth and goodness, and he sharply and harshly criticized those who preached harmless sermons about the size of Noah's ark. A defense of Pierpont would have been pointless by the time Parker wrote, so he attacked the Council for censuring Pierpont. Essentially, he charged that they blamed Pierpont for preaching as he should; and thereby he leveled another attack at the Unitarian establishment. (Of Parker's article on the Council in *The Dial* Margaret Fuller told Emerson, "It sold the number.") This article, *A Discourse of Religion,* and the South Boston sermon precipitated a meeting in January, 1843, of the Boston Association of Ministers.

Lengthy accounts, based on Parker's version of this meeting, are given in the biographies by Weiss, Frothingham, Chadwick, and Commager. Briefly, what occurred was that the Boston Association of Ministers had for several months been discussing Parker's actions of the past two years. When the article in *The Dial* prompted additional discussions, it was finally resolved to invite Parker to answer the charge against him. *A Discourse of Religion* was said to be "vehemently deistical" and not Christian. One member charged that the book and the article were offensive and "reflected on the members of the Association." Parker was invited to respond to these and other charges, but he was warned that the doctrines presented in the book were not to be discussed. According to all accounts of the meeting, Parker responded that he had to lecture in Boston and publish the book in order to be heard; that exchanges with most members of the Association had been closed to him. He denied that the book was Deistical and began to argue this and other matters, but he was again told that the doctrines presented were not to be discussed.

Parker tried another tack; he assured the Association that he had asked others to write an article on the Hollis Street Council, and they refused; before sending it in, he asked others to read his article, and they did so. (In his journal he noted that three of them were present.) Failing to persuade the Association with this approach, Parker argued that this whole matter had begun not with the publication of the *Discourse* or with the article but with the South Boston sermon of two years before. At this point in the meeting the suggestion was made that Parker withdraw from the Association. Parker stood on the "right of free inquiry."[17] The discussion continued with charges that Parker and his book were not Christian.

About three hours after the discussion had begun, Cyrus A. Bartol stood to speak of Parker's sincerity; then Ezra S. Gannett rose; then Chandler Robbins. Parker left in tears. A few days later Robbins wrote to him praising him for his theological knowledge but doubting that he and Parker were the same sort of Christian. In his reply, Parker reiterated his purpose to stay in the Association until expelled. Parker had been confronted by the establishment—and had lost. They had shown him that they accepted him as a man but doubted and disagreed with all his works; he could not accept these terms. He continued to challenge them and yet to wonder why they shunned him.

Not long after this meeting Parker published his "translation" of De Wette, *A Critical and Historical Introduction to the Canonical Scriptures of the Old Testament*, "Translated and Enlarged" by Parker. The preface is dated August 24, 1843. Begun in about 1836 "at the suggestion of an eminent theologian, of the Orthodox denomination," probably Francis, this work is Parker's most erudite one. He considered calling it "Introduction on the Basis of De Wette"; for he condensed and expanded where he thought necessary, added a one hundred page appendix, removed notes, incorporated others into the text, added numerous footnotes of his own, translated many passages of Scripture, and even wrote whole essays he finally did not include. For Parker, De Wette stood "at the head of the liberal school of German critics"; since by 1840 the German saw the fifth edition of this work published.

Since Parker agreed with De Wette's approach to the Bible, he translated the following statement from De Wette's preface without comment:

Since the object of an introduction to the Bible is the history of the Bible, its scientific character is historico-critical; that is, the Bible is to be considered as an historical phenomena, and entirely subject to the laws of historical inquiry. The consideration of it in a religious view—that is, according to the dogma of inspiration and revelation—falls within the department of introduction only so far as this dogma is connected with the history of the origin of the Bible. This dogma itself, therefore, is likewise to be treated historically. However, the introductory treatment of the history of the canon must turn out differently from the dogmatic history of the same, because the critical principle preponderates in the former.

Parker knew full well that this was not the method accepted by most English and American theologians who insisted "that the books of the Bible should be examined from a religious point of view, declaring that *dogmatic theology* is the touchstone, wherewith we are to decide between the true and the false, the genuine and the spurious."

Parker had accepted the German approach in theology, just as his fellow Transcendentalists had at least ostensibly accepted German literature and philosophy. He might have translated De Wette without comment, but he could not do so. In addition to complementing the original with notes and translations, he continually intruded. For example, he translated from the original, "If the introduction is treated in the genuine spirit of criticism, it has, then, the further advantage of awakening [a] the spirit of historical investigation in theology." His footnote reads, " [a] [*Keeping awake* (*Wach zu erhalten*) is the author's literal meaning; but it would scarcely apply in America, where this spirit is only known to be feared.]" [18] The comment is superfluous to a translation of the work, but Parker's pride and his combative spirit would not permit him merely to translate the German's work.

In a recent study of Parker's theology, John Edward Dirks comments at length on this work. Since the German's erudition encouraged Parker to collect an enormous library and to read most of De Wette's sources, Parker's research provided an excellent education for the young scholar. In the end, Parker produced "a comprehensive encyclopedia of Biblical learning," though not an original contribution. With it, Parker became one of the "first in America to conceive of Biblical criticism as a field of scientific inquiry" and "a prophet of historical criticism in the New World." None of the leading American critics of Parker's time accepted this approach, however. Using it, Parker was led to conclude, for example, that the Book of Ruth is a "narrative . . .

first circulated orally and later enriched in literary significance by the added genealogy of David." And,

The book of Esther was interpreted as a "patriotic romance" primarily fictional in character. Parker's conclusion that it was compiled after the destruction of the Persian monarchy was supported by an unusually extensive study of characteristically later literary forms; he cited numerous illustrations of the interpolation of Persian words into the Hebrew text. This conclusion, with the others regarding "the so-called books of history," illustrates Parker's tendency to exercise private judgment and his interest in some of the most technical aspects of Biblical criticism.[19]

The work is a significant achievement showing immense erudition; few, if any, other Americans could have done it.

This work of Parker's came as an anticlimax to his battles with his fellow Unitarians; it could further offend them but not more deeply. Parker's other work was a public challenge to both laity and clergy, but this abstruse book would not be read by the public; and it could scarcely be understood by many clergymen. This scholarly, erudite work played virtually no part in the fight between Parker and the Unitarian establishment, but it is unquestionably one of Parker's greatest achievements. Though it occupied much of his time for almost seven years, it foreshadowed little of the work of his later life.

V Europe

The year 1843 also marked his good fortune, through the kindness of a friend in West Roxbury, of being able to go to Europe for almost a year. He had published, he had preached, he had met his Unitarian elders; now he needed rest. And Parker's joy in going to Europe cannot be overestimated. The trip meant that he would see not only the places but also the people he had read about and those whose books he had studied; and De Wette would be one of them. On September 9 Parker sailed on the *Ashburton*, but his year's education began in New York where he visited the Court of Sessions and the Tombs. In the court he saw a Negro whom Parker thought exemplified the ills of society. The man had been a slave who had escaped into a society where he had no rights, and here he was on trial for beating his wife. In the Tombs Parker saw a man who had been put in jail for drunkenness. He noted that, if the man had been drunk at the

Astor House and gone to bed, the police would not have arrested him.

He continued to observe such social-economic ills on board ship. Parker was among the 30 passengers in the cabin rather than among the 160 in the forecastle. He recognized the same sort of social-economic division existed in the cities where "it is thundered in our ears each moment, but in little despotism, a ship, you see the whole thing more clearly, because more compendiously. There must be a cure for this terrible evil. What is it?" Seeking solutions to the problems, he found the answer in religion and in the application of religion to life. "This is the field in which I design to labor." He resolved to do this work and to discharge the debt of his year's travel in these ways: "1. To work in behalf of temperance, education, a change in the social fabric, so that the weak shall not be the slaves of the strong. "2. To show that religion belongs to man's nature, that it demands piety and morality (the inward sentiment, the outward action), and theology (the mediator between the two.)"[20] And he planned an introduction to the New Testament, a popular introduction to the Old Testament, and a history of the development of religion.

These plans were not wholly forgotten. Though he never wrote any of these books, he did follow the other lines of work he established for himself. Especially, he labored in behalf of the weak—the slaves, the poor, the intemperate—and to show the place and function of religion in society and in the life of the individual. In these endeavors there was a change of emphasis from the course Parker had been pursuing in the years since he had left Harvard, for the heightened social consciousness demonstrated is not that of the scholar who had translated De Wette, or that of the young man who had once coveted the position of dean in the Divinity School. He fought on new ground, but he continued to fight against the establishment.

Parker's European experiences, especially his own accounts of them, are worth recounting briefly for what they reveal about the man—his interests, his prejudices, and his enthusiasms. Freed from the compulsion of producing weekly sermons, articles, and lectures, he plunged with equal energy into knowing Europe and its people. The record of his activity suggests the amount of energy Parker normally spent on his religious interests and would soon devote to social reform. But such speculation is unfaithful to the man whose sense of righteous duty prevented him from choosing another profession, from leaving the pulpit, and from succumbing to pressures to give up his theology, his Abolitionism, and his crusades against injustice. Europe became for Parker another book to be read with interest, enthusiasm, and goodwill in order to judge its parts with righteousness.

After Parker had landed at Liverpool he began to travel as voraciously as he read. In his journal and in his letters he recorded meeting John J. Tayler, a Unitarian minister; then, during dinner with him and John Newman, they discuss particularly Plato and Aristotle; and Parker is the only one of the three who likes Plato's *Republic*. He admires Newman. Parker goes to Manchester and thinks of Cromwell's men, sees the room where Shakespeare was born; sees Carlyle. In Paris, Parker attends lectures on all manner of things and records notes on all of them in his journal. He seems in good humor: "I saw a Frenchman kiss his horse in the street to-day; a fine, noble horse it was, too. I also came up and paid my respects, though not with my lips." [21]

Like most Americans, Parker comments endlessly on the Catholic Church and the beggars. Every place he mentions brings to his mind the history of centuries. The particularly provoking, catacombs of Rome remind him of the simplicity of the early church and the importance of martyrdom. With some other Americans, he has a short audience with the Pope. He visits Florence, Leghorn, and Venice; but only the Catholic Church holds his attention. More than a hint of intolerance appears when he writes of saints, relics, church, priests, and he is not above recording hints of scandals involving priests. He virtually summarizes his judgment of the city in this sentence from a letter: "If I wanted to convert a fop to Christianity, I think I would send him to Rome; but if I wanted to put a philosopher in the Catholic Church, I would send him anywhere but to Rome." [22]

From Italy, Parker makes his way towards Germany. In Berlin, as in Paris, he attends lectures, hearing Karl Werder on logic and Friedrich Schelling on Offenbarungs-Philosophie talking about Immanuel Kant, Johann Fichte, and Geroge W. Hegel. Here too he hears Johann Vatke, Carl L. Michelet, August Twesten, and Henrich Steffens. Few places give him such obvious pleasure as Wittenberg, the home of Luther. In Halle he meets and hears Friederich A. Tholuck; in Heidelberg, "all the notable professors." When he journeys to Tubingen to see the men he most admires, he sees Heinrich Ewald and delights in his idea, that the Bible seems more worthwhile when it is studied with more freedom. And he hears lectures by Ferdinand Baur, Reinhold Schmidt, and De Wette. De Wette, whom he finds charming though more conservative than in his younger years, takes him to the library to look at manuscripts, including one by Erasmus. Parker glories in Germany, especially in Berlin, where he thinks it a *"disguise"* to be a great man, since such men are so common. He describes the city: "For the moving part of it, imagine 1000 hackney coaches, the drivers with cows'-tails on top of their caps, 100 private carriages, 400 drags for beer, 150 carts, and wagons for other business, 30,000 soldiers, 1650 students, 100 professors (it will take a day to imagine them all), a King, Baron Von Humboldt, and 270,000 others."[23] Parker's fascination with the theologians is in part due to the innocuous battles he has fought in America, but he finds now the controversies over Hegel more exciting. From Berlin he goes to Zurich, Bonn, Cologne, Antwerp, London, Liverpool, and home.

Parker sought out and talked with Europeans of great significance to him. He recorded his impressions of these men and some of their ideas; but he said little about landscapes, houses, and individuals he saw in the streets. In most of his letters and in his journals there is great humor and spirit. That he learned much in the lecture halls, the studies, the libraries, or elsewhere is doubtful; but that he experienced Europe with gusto there is no doubt. For Parker the great world beyond Boston was the one that he wished to know better and that he desired to know him. The effervescence of his notes and letters written while abroad reveal by contrast the pain and heaviness he often felt in America from his unwanted battles with his fellow clergymen. But he could not escape the world he had made for himself in Massachusetts.

VI *Boston*

Shortly after Parker's return to the United States, new conflicts arose. In September, 1844, he began to preach again. In November, John T. Sargent arranged to exchange with Parker and as a result was forced to resign from the Suffolk Street Chapel which was governed by the Benevolent Fraternity of Churches, an official Unitarian body. Though the case was difficult because Sargent came from a wealthy family and had been a successful minister among the poor, the Benevolent Fraternity quickly resolved to ask for his resignation. The following month, Parker, who was still a member of the Boston Ministerial Association, preached the Thursday lecture at the First Church, Dr. N. L. Frothingham's, on the day after Christmas. His subject was "The Relation of Jesus to his Age and the Ages."

The Thursday lecture was a revered institution, though it was no longer very popular. It was usually attended, according to O. B. Frothingham, who knew it first hand, by "A score or two of venerable women [who] glided silently in at the hour of eleven, and took their seats, well provided with bottles of *sal-volatile* against the probable effect of the discourse." A choir was usually assembled for the occasion; a student organist occupied the seat before that instrument; and Octavius Brooks Frothingham, Dr. Frotningham's son and the future biographer of Parker, pumped the bellows. The younger Frothingham recalled, "None came but saints, and these came not with jubilant feet."[24]

But on the December 26 the church was so crowded that those who came late could find no seats. Most listeners carried away with them not the positive praise which Parker gave to Christ but the denial of the supernatural. Though Parker largely repeated ideas he had previously stated, the reaction was immediate. Parker could not be forced out of the Boston Ministerial Association; this they had learned before. And he would not withdraw. But Dr. Frothingham devised another plan which would achieve the desired end with respect to the Thursday lecture: the affair would simply be returned to the direction of the minister of the First Church—himself. The Thursday lecture did not long survive this action.

A month after the lecture at the First Church, Parker exchanged pulpits with James Freeman Clarke. The sermon, "The Excellence of Goodness," really did not matter; people reacted to the exchange. Clarke lost fifteen of the best families—socially and financially—from his small congregation at a time when he was trying to build a "free church", a difficult task under any circumstances. Two from the congregation of Clarke's Church of the Disciples, Benjamin H. Greene and John A. Andrew, later the governor of the state, had gone to both Clarke and Parker to advise them against the exchange. But Clarke, who pursued his course, made it clear to his congregation that he was performing a duty. As usual at a Parker sermon, the church was filled, though not with Clarke's people. The following night, January 27, the Ministerial Association met at Cyrus A. Bartol's to discuss the expulsion of Parker; but again the members could not agree to force him out. A few days before, January 22, 1845, a group of men in Boston *had* passed a resolution: "That the Rev. Theodore Parker shall have a chance to be heard in Boston." They obtained, a theater, the Melodeon, and Parker preached his first sermon there on February 16, 1845. This occasion was the beginning of a new and even busier life.

About the time he came first to preach regularly in Boston, Parker, having decided to confront the Association publicly, wrote "A Letter to the Boston Association of Congregational Ministers Touching Certain Matters of Their Theology." In it he referred to the several years of controversy, to the meetings held concerning his membership in the association, and to his exclusion from the Thursday lecture. As usual, he protested that he was not complaining. (How often his pride trampled his humility.) Ostensibly searching for the Unitarian theological position, Parker reviewed the theological pattern of American Unitarianism—its supposed liberalism and willingness to let a man find his theology and its position on the place of religion in life and of Christ in religion. He reminded Unitarians of the time when their denial of the Trinity had caused them to be denied the name of Christian and accused them of now adopting the same course, since only five ministers had exchanged pulpits with him since the South Boston sermon. He recalled the Hollis Street Council and the expulsion of Sargent.

Returning to the problems of the denomination, Parker pointed out its lack of a creed for ministers, students, and congregations; and he wondered how he could have gone beyond the limits of Unitarianism since—supposedly—no limits had been established. He assumed heresy to be the main charge against him, and asked Unitarians what is their orthodoxy: "As I try to comprehend it, I feel I am looking at something dim and undefined. It changes color, and it changes shape: now it seems a mountain; then it appears like a cloud." He charged that to accuse him they—each one of them—must know their orthodoxy, have investigated his work, and agreed that it is heretical.

Parker concluded with pages of questions for them to answer.

He asked for their definitions of salvation, miracle, inspiration, revelation—concepts Parker defined again and again in his sermons and books. He presented queries about authority, the truth of the Scriptures, the inspiration of the authors, the facts of the miracles, the prophecies of the Old Testament, the character of the apostles, the nature of Jesus, the supernatural quality of Jesus and His resurrection, and baptism and communion.[25] Parker was throwing down the gauntlet before his Boston Unitarian brethren, and he could have expected no answer. But, in his stubborn and naive fashion, he was attempting to clarify the issues and publicly to prepare his own way in the city. Now all men could judge—at least that was the spirit in which he wrote.

Though it has usually been said that there was no reply to Parker's letter to the Boston Ministerial Association and his other attacks on Unitarian doctrine, Dr. N. L. Frothingham's "Deism or Christianity," a series of four discourses of 1845, and other sermons did fulfill that purpose. For example, Frothingham admitted that the Unitarians did at first deny various doctrines of orthodoxy, but he insisted that they did not reject all doctrines and all limits. While they promoted free inquiry, they did not forgo responsibility. Without some principle of exclusion, there would be no inclusion. He charged that Parker sometimes forgot that the Unitarians did believe in Christ as a mediator between God and man, and in the Bible as holy testimony. Parker, of course, did not forget these doctrines. He perhaps should have responded directly to Frothingham's charge that man was "approaching, as his last delusion, to the worship of himself" with the counterargument that Frothingham was describing Unitarian practice. Though there was a reluctance to resolve the real differences, they did exist. Frothingham believed, for example, that miracles were important proofs of the authenticity of Christianity; Parker disagreed.

In describing the conflict between his father, Dr. Frothingham, and others who formed the core of Boston Unitarianism, and Parker, the younger Frothingham suggested that Parker offended most by attacking traditions and the authority of the church that had established them: "If Parker could simply have shifted the basis of authority from the Bible to the Soul, without disturbing the traditions of faith, there might have been no contest in spite of his biting sarcasms." But even the younger Frothingham recognized the basic differences: Parker and other Transcendentalists accepted a philosophy "resting the origin of religious ideas on the native beliefs of the human reason, necessarily made light of outward evidences,—prophecy, miracle, authenticity of the Scriptures, narrative, mission, and saying of Jesus." According to him, Emerson and Ripley could hold and pronounce such beliefs without exciting opposition but Parker expressed these beliefs so directly and with such sharpness and aggressiveness that he could not be ignored.

The younger Frothingham forgot the reactions to Emerson's Divinity School Address and to various sermons and publications of Ripley. Furthermore, he neglected such accessory aspects as these: Emerson and Ripley left the church; the orthodox continued their attack on the Unitarians; many second-generation graduates of the Divinity School were supporting the new movement; the Unitarian churches were receiving much of their support from the conservative portions of Boston society. But, as Frothingham pointed out, none of these facts absolves Parker from the methods and tone he used. He recounted that when Parker found Ferdinand Baur—who was regarded as radical in his country as Parker was in Boston—preaching from a Lutheran pulpit in Germany, he was surprised; Baur, on the other hand, was amazed that Parker so publicly proclaimed his opinions: "They were conclusions of the study; surmises of scholarship; matters of literary concern; private speculations, not suitable for edification; questions for learning to decide, not for faith or feeling. But Parker could not understand this distinction."[26] Many of the Unitarians would have agreed with Baur that Parker opened the speculations of the study to the air. From Parker's point of view they were truths available to every man and not mere speculations for the study. Without realizing it, Parker had gone beyond his German mentors in his use of their methods and in the conclusions drawn from them.

The Unitarian Boston which Parker invaded in 1845 was that of Dr. Frothingham whom his son characterized as "a Unitarian of the old school. Dr. [William Ellery] Channing he took no interest in, and less than none in Theodore Parker. Emerson on the one side and Abner Kneeland on the other were about equally far from his sympathies." This assertion is not quite the truth since in 1845 Dr. Frothingham was defending his faith against the new views. But, certainly, he would have liked to ignore Parker, since he was a conservative who took no positive interest in reform politics or any other sort of radicalism. John Pierpont, whose views had been investigated by the Hollis Street Council, had raised ethical issues which had provoked the conservatives. The denomination represented the "religion of the educated, the refined, the scholarly, the wealthy, the leaders of society. Great merchants, politicians, statesmen, judges were apt to be members of Unitarian congregations. This influence was strongly conservative of the existing order, and threw the weight of public opinion against agitation or reform."[27] This establishment Parker somewhat unwittingly attacked on theological grounds. Though he saw Unitarianism as a mode of interpretation and as a body of ill-defined doctrines, it was also ministers and congregations, vested interests, a whole community. With an uncanny skill Parker soon provoked that community in all its aspects.

CHAPTER 4

The Mature Reformer

T heodore Parker had entered the decade of the 1840's with the substantial hope of becoming a theological scholar of note; he hoped to reform Unitarianism, to be another William Ellery Channing. But in less than five years, Parker recognized the opposition which prevented him from altering the sect. After the religious conflict had been established, but by no means resolved, Parker came to Boston, preached to thousands, became a popular lecturer, and edited the *Massachusetts Quarterly Review.* The great preacher was able to spread his ideas through the land, but he was not so persuasive as he wished nor was he able to show his readers and listeners that everything he said and did was in the name and spirit of the modified Unitarian religion that he preached.

I *Boston and a New Congregation*

On January 22, 1845, a group of laymen resolved to invite him to speak, and on February 16, 1845, he gave his first sermon in the Melodeon where he continued to preach until 1852 when the congregation moved to the Music Hall. The services in Boston were so well attended that in November, 1845, the Twenty-eighth Congregational Society was formed. Parker later recalled the strange atmosphere of the Melodeon: "As I have stood here, I have often seen the spangles of opera dancers, who beguiled the previous night, lying on the floor beside me." And he re-membered the others who performed during the week: "Dancing monkeys and 'Ethiopian serenaders,' making vulgar merriment out of the ignorance and wretchedness of the American slave. . . ."[1] But this atmosphere did not adversely affect Parker's enormous success in Boston.

Parker had not been quick to move there and leave his West Roxbury congregation, and for a time he preached in both the town and the city. In December, 1845, he was invited to become the first permanent minister of the Twenty-eighth Congregational

Society. On January 3, 1846, when he formally told the West
Roxbury congregation that he was leaving them the second Sunday
in February, he blamed those clergymen who would not exchange
with him for forcing him to move to the city. However much he
valued his rural church, he did want a Boston platform. In part,
his purpose in coming to Boston was to establish a church which
would realize his notion of the ideal. His installation sermon
was "The Idea of a Christian Church." Speaking now to his own
"free church," he defined the church as "a body of men and women
united together in a common desire of religious excellence, and
with a common regard for Jesus of Nazareth, regarding him as
the noblest example of morality and religion." Its proper activity
should include the duty of reform throughout society—to act
against war and slavery, to combat crime and its causes, and to
improve prison conditions. The church, as the primary institution,
should lead society and be willing to accept the ideas of science
and philosophy.[2] While others might have been ready to acquiesce
in the relegation of the church to matters of religion in the narrow-
est sense, Parker wished to broaden its function.

His congregation, with as many as 7000 on the register (and
a solid core of 500), included individuals from the most diverse
groups. Many flaunted Boston society in order to attend the
church, and a few habitually came after the service began and
left before its close to avoid observation. Parker's ambition of
preaching to a large congregation with important members was,
in this respect, satisfied; for, among those who attended his
services, were reformers such as William L. Garrison; Samuel
G. Howe and his wife, Julia Ward Howe; and politicians such as
Salmon P. Chase, John P. Hale, and Charles Sumner. If not the
most distinguished congregation in Boston, it was the largest;
and, to the orthodox, its preacher the most notorious. Though
to many Parker was not of Boston and never would be, he was
in Boston. He felt himself to be in the seat of Northern power,
preaching in the city where the course of society and government
might be shaped.

In January, 1847, he moved his family to a house on Exeter
Place where his yard adjoined that of Wendell Phillips, a leading
Abolitionist. With George Cabot, the orphan brought up by the
childless Parkers, and Miss Hannah Stevenson, another member
of the household, Theodore and Lydia established their Boston
home. The top floor of the house was the library, though

there were books in every room and hall—he eventually owned 25,000—and the whole house was the reception hall. He lived two blocks from the Boston Common where he could escape to a city version of the country. Parker never could avoid this passion for going to the country when he could and for enjoying the trees and flowers of Boston when he could not. But living in the city gave him more opportunity to exercise the friendly philanthropy for which he was known.

If Parker is judged solely by his published sermons and lectures, the "faculty of affection," as he called it, that he expected in others would seem absent in him. But his great kindness to all who came for help reveals the quality in abundance. Parker, who clearly expected his journal to be read by others, recorded the visitors of one day: After attending to matters of the home and siting down to finish a sermon, Parker greets a Negro who wants to borrow money; soon after him, an orthodox minister from Ohio seeks money to start a free church; then a minister comes to borrow a book and to talk about the immortality of the soul according to Zoroaster. Silas Lamson brings two farm machines for Parker to look at; a Mrs. M. and then Greeley Curtis come to visit; Parker's good friend, Mrs. Sally Russell, stays from five to nine.

Parker did not, however, always lay everything aside while talking to his visitors. Frothingham gave an account of Parker's cutting the pages of a book while he talked to a friend. When he laid down the paper knife and the book, the visitor remarked that he could not have read it while cutting the pages. Parker challenged, "Try me, and judge."[3] The reading and writing continued as they had in West Roxbury, but the visiting and the correspondence, increased. Frothingham found 948 copies of Parker's letters in seven volumes, only a portion of all he wrote. To one friend, Edouard Desor, the Swiss geologist, Parker wrote the equivalent of 300 folio pages.

The Twenty-eighth Congregational Society outgrew the spacious Melodeon and moved in 1852 to the Music Hall, built by the Harvard Musical Association for $100,000. It could hold 3,000 persons and did on some occasions for Parker's sermons. These hour-long addresses were on literature, politics, history, or science, and they were part of the simple services of prayers and hymns.

The large audiences came to hear what Parker would say rather than to listen to the man's style which was sometimes simple and repetitive. (Parker thought these characteristics helped to clarify the ideas.) The audiences who came to hear such sermons behaved differently from those of other Boston churches. The congregation did not dress as people did for other churches; they came and went during the service, sat where they wished in the free pews, and read newspapers before the services.

O. B. Frothingham considered Parker a "man of the people" and the "greatest [preacher] of his generation."[4] A great preacher he surely was, as the size of his audiences attest; but the number of lectures also reflect his fame: he gave forty in the 1844—45 season; ninety eight in the winter of 1855. His potential influence on his generation was enormous. The sermons, spoken and published, were heard or read by thousands; his articles were read by many more; his lectures were well attended.

II *The Mexican War*

About the time that Parker began preaching regularly in Boston, he commenced new reform work. He was, after all, a reformer in all his interests. Working from his principles, he set out to convince others of the current wrongs and the appropriate remedies. His reform work was to him always part of his effort toward the realization of absolute religion—his name for the religion he preached and practiced—but he also recognized that new opportunity was offered by the pulpit in Boston. From this time, half of his sermons were on reform.

One of Parker's early efforts concerned the problem of war. Late in 1844 he noted that the issues of slavery and the admission of Texas were interwoven; in fact, war over Texas would be "A war for slavery!" In 1845 he wrote to historian George Bancroft, then a member of the Cabinet as secretary of the navy, about the possibility of war with England and the admission of Texas as a slave state. Though Parker protested that he did not believe the rumors of war which he had heard, he pleaded with Bancroft to recall the costs of war in money and in lives and in "the confusion it brings into the minds, and hearts too, of men." War with England "would retard the progress of man full half a century."[5]

Parker used cost and progress again and again in his arguments. While he perhaps knew the rhetorical effect, he was not merely appealing to an audience; for him, cost and progress were crucial considerations. The progress of the nation toward an industrial democracy and a utopian state were dreams he shared with many of his countrymen, and slavery represented an obstacle to each. In calling upon Bancroft to block the admission of Texas as a slave state, he reminded the historian of his lecture on Roman slavery and of his knowledge as a philosopher and as a historian of the meaning of slavery. Parker urged him to speak out even if it cost him his seat in the Cabinet, and he warned him that, if he did not support his words with his deeds, he would be remembered for the deeds rather than the books. Had Parker known Bancroft and politics better, he would have realized the decision about the admission of Texas had already been made.

Parker's failure to prevent the Mexican War through his appeals to Bancroft and others did not stop him from condemning it. For example, in "A Sermon of War" which he preached at the Melodeon on June 7, 1846, he continued his attack.[6] Using his favorite method of approaching a subject in its most general context before addressing himself to specifics, he spoke first of the place of war in civilization and Christianity: war belongs to a lower state of civilization than that of the nineteenth century; and, if war is right, then Christianity is wrong. However, God sometimes permits sins, chiefly war, to advance civilization; but such a conflict still remains a sin. Aggressive war is particularly bad. From a secular point of view, war has a high cost in money and men; the soldier is unproductive; and the money could be better spent. (After the war Parker calculated the United States' cost at $200 million, equal to the cost of building railroads across Panama and from the Mississippi River to the Pacific Ocean, and 15,000 dead out of 150,000 American troops.)[7] War is only acceptable for a captive people or for self-protection or against falsehood. But none of these conditions exist in the Mexican War. If war is usually wrong, and if the war with Mexico is clearly wrong, what should the citizens do? Though the people cannot stop the war at once, they can refuse to pay taxes; and they can also hold public protest meetings. Either course would be in the rebellious American tradition and might stop the war.

Early in the following year, 1847, Parker continued his protests at an antiwar meeting in a speech in which he accused the government of waging the war only to extend slavery.[8] He repeated his advice to refuse to pay taxes, and he advised men not to volunteer. Acknowledging that his speech might be termed treasonable, Parker declared that real treason is to know the government is wrong and to accept the wrong. His efforts to prevent and later to halt the war might have prepared him for other frustrations in trying to move the government and the people.

III *Poverty and Wealth*

During the 1840's as Parker devoted more time to social and political issues and less to theology, he came to know the city better and became interested in the problems of poverty, crime, prostitution, education, and temperance. Using a statistical approach which he later used almost excessively in his antislavery addresses, he analyzed the situation in Boston. To identify the class of people living in poverty, he described the class structure as comprised of three groups: those who live on their capital, those who live by mental or manual skill, and those who must live by their muscles alone. The poor, who make up the whole of the last class, pay more for the necessities than do the wealthy and are forced to live without hope in a society which values wealth so highly. Their condition is so bad that not even mortality is a curse. One of their most common vices is drunkenness, as Parker proved through the number of gallons sold and the number of liquor outlets. To support the statistics, he told stories such as this: "one of the city police, on Sunday morning, between the hours of twelve and two, in walking from Cornhill Square to Cambridge Street, passed more than one hundred persons more or less drunk!"[9]

Parker's ultimate remedy was a more Christian society established through the efforts of all men. Though this vague solution is hardly impressive as a basis for action, the analysis and presentation of the problems are noteworthy. He did not offer the utopian communities such as Brook Farm as guides or models. His solution may have been visionary, but his identification of the problems was more realistic than that of many of his contemporaries.

In a later sermon he specifically rejected the ideas of the utopians, while sympathizing with their hope.[10] For Parker, "Poverty is the dark side of modern society." His analysis of the problem frequently presages the judgments offered a century later. "On the whole, the price of things has come down and the price of work has gone up. Yet still there are the poor, there is want, there is misery, there is starvation." And the recognition of permanent poverty can be seen in his writing: "The old poverty is parent of new poverty." Some classes are kept down: "The blacks in New England are despised and frowned down."

Poverty can only be eliminated when its causes are removed. The alternative is revolution: "If powerful men will not write justice with black ink, on white paper, ignorant and violent men will write it on the soil, in letters of blood, and illuminate their rude legislation with burning castles, palaces, and towns [in Europe and America]." Parker's program for eliminating poverty includes tenements at reasonable rent, more work, cheaper food, prevention of beggary, promotion of temperance, and opportunity for education. His suggestion for housing may seem familiar to a generation a hundred years later; he suggests that "to hire money at six per cent., and rent the houses built therewith at eight per cent., would cost less than to support the poor [with public funds]." Analyses such as these justify regarding Parker as a forerunner of such men as Edward Bellamy and Norman Thomas.

The causes of poverty he identified in Boston and in England are hereditary class, ability, family size, intemperance, and lack of development. In other countries, he found different causes: sometimes the land is too poor to support the population; in Mexico, the race itself promotes poverty; in Spain, much is spent though little earned; and in other countries the laws curb freedom or create inequitable patterns of income distribution. As usual, for Parker, the uniqueness of America caused unique problems.

He was not always practical, nor was he always realistic in his view of a problem. Examining crime, he concluded that the criminal code was based on force rather than love. His only solution was that there must be basic changes in society before crime could be eliminated. Even then, he admitted, the "criminals in soul," the foes of society, could not be reformed.[11] In sermons such as this Parker was working out the problem and its solution in his sermon rather than presenting a carefully reasoned analysis. The pressure of preparing weekly sermons and of attending to all his other activities was sometimes too great.

Parker did not concern himself only with the lower classes of society in his analyses in the 1840's. Though he never completed a description of any of the three classes he distinguished, he spent much time on the wealthy who constituted for Parker the power class of the society. Beginning with a set of categories—producers, manufacturers, consumers, and merchants—Parker subdivided merchants into producers, manufacturers, and traders. This approach was unproductive, so he discarded these divisions to treat merchants as one class. (Parker was so eager to discover knowledge through classification that he often presents such a scheme only to disregard it immediately. Another man might have used such a method in the notes for a sermon but then omitted it from the final version. The carelessness was, in part, due to the haste in which he often completed his sermons.)

Parker's analysis of the merchant class is important for an understanding of Parker's view of his society. He defined the merchants as those who buy and sell, but he later described them as those who use other men's labor. Though ambiguous about the ethics of this process of accumulation, he found it "unavoidable." Since "wealth is power," the merchants make up the power class of the society. Though merchants have existed since the Middle Ages, they have never controlled society as they do in America. In Europe, the clergy, the military, and the nobles have the power function reserved for merchants in America. Here their power gives them the control of politics and the church, but Parker did not analyze the use and methods of the control.

Since wealth is valued so highly and can give power, the desire for wealth becomes primary. To illustrate the condition of those without wealth, Parker told a story which is virtually his own:

The poor man's son, however well-born, struggling for a superior education, obtains his culture at a monstrous cost; with the sacrifice of pleasure, comfort, the joys of youth, often of eyesight and health. He must do two men's work at once—learn and teach at the same time. He learns all by his soul, nothing from his circumstances. If he have not an iron body as well as an iron head, he dies in that experiment of the cross. The land is full of poor men who have attained a superior culture, but carry a crippled body through all their life [sic]. The rich man's son needs not that terrible trial. He learns from circumstances, not his soul. The air about him contains a diffused element of thought. He learns without knowing it. Colleges open their doors; accomplished teachers stand ready; science and art, music and literature, come at the rich man's call. All the outward means of educating, refining, elevating a child, are to be had for money, and for money alone.

Then, too, wealth gives men a social position, which nothing else save the rarest genius can obtain, and which that, in the majority of cases lacking the commercial conscience, is sure not to get. Many men prize this social rank above everything else, even above justice and a life unstained.

Parker could scarcely have written this without an awareness of its personal implications. He begrudged the cost of his education and his lack of social position, but he had difficulty in criticizing the system since he could offer no realistic alternative. He could only assert that justice and virtue should be valued above wealth and position.

In Parker's view, wealth should bring responsibility; but he did not find this to be the case. The employed are "at the employer's mercy. Perhaps this is unavoidable; for one wishes to sell his work dear, the other to get it cheap as he can." Since to legislate on these matters is impossible, only conscience and Christianity could regulate the relations between these two classes. In the South, slavery is a result of irresponsibility; in the North, a similar condition is created by paying men only a subsistence wage. Christianity, asserting that all men are brothers and that the strong must help the weak, dictates another course. However, merchants do not follow this path; instead, they favor laws which help only themselves and often oppress their employees. But Parker recognized that this powerful class could do good as well as ill; it could employ men, start industries, control rivers—and even build the industrial democracy which Parker envisions. Through political control this group could pass laws to promote freedom, end slavery, establish schools, help the weak, and prevent poverty and crime: "They can thus help organize society after the Christian idea, and promote the kingdom of heaven." The duty of the merchant class is clear.

But, instead, this class turns away from all reforms; and even supports the extension of slavery. The merchants do not favor temperance nor the abolition of capital punishment and of imprisonment for debt. They foster the causes of poverty and of indirect taxation which is harder on the poor than on the rich. That the clergymen are on the side of such power is most disturbing to Parker. That trade takes precedence over the arts causes the paucity of American literature: "Politics represent the morals of the controlling class," and politics represents immorality. Parker's mythical baron who cheats, lies, steals, favors slave trade, causes poverty, and sells rum, "knows no right, only power; no man but self; no God but his calf of gold."[12] Parker protested that he did not wish to set rich against poor, and clearly he did not want nor expect a society without merchants. He pleaded for Christian merchants; he preached against non-Christian action, against a morality of political and economic power; and he was the liberal attacking the misuse of power and the perversion of virtue.

Parker's comments on industrial democracy are important to an understanding of his significance, and they have occasionally been presented in a misleading manner. Parker, like Orestes Brownson, did attack the very notion of a society in which the values of property and wealth are primary. A society permeated by the values of business could only be—to the righteous Parker— an immoral society. The moral utopia that Parker expected on earth could hardly be established if commerce ruled.

However, to emphasize Parker's opposition to the merchant class—the merchant system and the merchants' values—is to overlook another aspect of his thought. Late in his life, in 1858, he argued, "I will not say that our industrial democracy secures all the advantages of each other form of government, and escapes from all their ills. It is a new experiment, not complete nor perfect." In other words, it was not perfect but it was better than other systems. A few years earlier he had predicted, "the industrial democracy rooted in the soil of God's world, obedient to God's laws, will rise a strong and flame-like flower." In the same year he had said, "That is the first part of our scheme—we are aiming to found an industrial State." He continued, "It would be a fair spectacle,—a great industrial commonwealth, spread over half the continent, and folding in its bosom one-fortieth of God's whole family!"

To explain the phrase "industrial democracy" Parker once broke it down into its component parts, pointing out that the first aim was an industrial state and the second a democracy—"the government of all, by all, for all." While the first could create a highly stratified society, the second demanded equalities that prohibited such stratification. So, Parker, while he saw and feared some consequences of an industrial state, thought that a democracy could alleviate them. An industrial democracy could furnish the economic and political bases upon which a utopian state might be built. Like so many American liberals who would come later, Parker worried over the evils of a capitalist state and looked to the benefits of democracy to balance them. In most respects he resembles the New Deal Democrat more than the American Socialist. But always he was righteous.

Questions of values and morality in society are discussed in other sermons. In one, Parker said that the morals of Boston were those of trade because commerce was to Boston what the church was to Rome, and what the court was to Saint Petersburg. The love of money surpassed the love of truth or justice. Yet he claimed the moral condition of Boston had been improving, and to demonstrate this improvement he quoted the General Court of Massachusetts, Cotton Mather, John Norton, John Cotton and, most frequently, Increase Mather on the conditions of piety in Puritan Massachusetts. (Mather thought there was "a deluge of profaneness" and lamented "the degeneracy and departing glory of New England.") Parker justified his equating piety with morality with the assertion, "The piety of this age must manifest itself in morality." Hence, for him, the moral condition of Boston reflected its piety.

To continue the improvement, a change in the relations between capital and labor was necessary so that poverty and crime would be lessened, drunkenness diminshed. In Parker's continual search for ways to deal with crime, he suggested that one solution might be to make jails "moral hospitals." Though prostitution was mentioned in most of his sermons on social and economic conditions, it was treated as a result of poverty, not as a crime or as immorality.

In weaving his portrait of the society of Boston, Parker worked as his ideal historian would: he examined all aspects of the culture—trade, morality, religion, politics, the press. He evaluated what he called the spiritual condition of the city. Equating spiritual condition with piety permitted him to describe the changing religious beliefs and devotion of the citizens. He found two types of piety—the "conventional standard" established by sects to include church attendance and belief in a set of doctrines and the "natural standard" found "in the natural form of morality." By the first standard there was less and less piety as fewer and fewer believed in the Trinity, in divine inspiration of Scripture, in the depravity of man, and so forth. Skepticism was more common, for men attended two or three lectures a week but skipped the Sunday sermon.

The Unitarians were, to Parker, responsible for having undermined the conventional piety while not promoting the natural. The members of that sect "were kept together, not so much by an agreement and unity of opinion among themselves, as by a unity of opposition from without; it was not the hooks on their shields that held the legion together with even front, but the pressure of hostile shields crowded upon them from all sides." So concerned were they with their enemies that they forgot about themselves.

To reiterate what the piety of modern Boston was to be: "The piety of this age must manifest itself in morality, and appear in a church where the priests are men of active mind and active hand; men of ideals, who commune with God and man through faith and works, finding no truth is hostile to their creed, no goodness foreign to their litany, no piety discordant with their psalm." Rarely did Parker state his own belief in his function as a minister so concisely and with such clear reference to society and to religion. From the pulpit he hoped "to set forth absolute religion, the ideal religion of human nature, free piety, free goodness, free thought." He asked his congregation, "Let your piety become natural life, your divinity become humanity." [13] What began as a sermon on the conditions in the city ended with a description of what Parker expected of himself and his congregation. Characteristically, he thought out what he expected of himself and of them; and he stated his expectations with the assurance of his grandfather: "If they mean to have war, then let it begin here."

IV   Education

With the other Transcendentalists, Parker believed education to be a key to the improvement of men. For him, as for Emerson and Thoreau, education could not be divorced from the purpose of human life which Parker defined—"to form a manly character, to get the best development of body and of spirit,—of mind, conscience, heart, soul. This is the end: all else is the means." [14] The scholar is particularly important in developing men and nation since he represents "the higher modes of human consciousness . . . and truth, justice, beauty, philanthropy, and religion—the highest facts of human experience. . . ." In serving this purpose the scholar "must be common, but not vulgar, and, as a star, must dwell apart from the vulgarity of the selfish and the low." Simply in being these things the scholar paid society for his education.

Though America might lack the European aristocracy, it had both an aristocracy of wealth and a "natural aristocracy"; the scholars formed the latter; and though not boasting, he clearly placed himself among them. In describing American scholars Parker said they were more "metaphysical" than the English, since they were ready to welcome Transcendentalism from Germany and France: "This fact ["Calvinism bears metaphysical fruit in New England."] modifies still more the function of the duty of the scholar. It determines him to ideas, to facts for the ideas they cover, not so much to the past as the future, to the past only that he may guide the present and construct the future. He is to take his run in the past to acquire the momentum of history, his stand in the present, and leap into the future." There was scarcely room for the non-Transcendentalist scholar. Moving past facts to reach ideas, moving past the present to reach the future, characterize good Transcendentalist methodology. But the scholar had a duty to others also: "The test of the scholar's power is his ability to raise men in their development." [15] Having been elevated, the scholar had the duty to elevate others. Parker's prescription was his own medicine. Though his sermon on the American scholar is weaker than Emerson's, weaker even than George William Curtis's lecture, Parker's life—in his own view—demonstrates his conception of that ideal.

The scholar and the state cooperate to educate men, but each functions on a different level. As one of the rights of the people is to be educated, so one of the functions of the state is to assure this right. Broad education is necessary in a democracy so that men may vote wisely and be able to hold office. But beyond any political purpose, the individual has a human right to "the best culture," one which can be gained only through education. Parker's conception of education was based on the broadest definition; "Education is the developing and furnishing of the faculties of man." [16] Education is not merely vocational, not merely secular, though Parker recognized the values of these as he asked for free college education for all. When he included the "faculties of man" in his definition, he referred to the moral and religious as well as to the secular. Parker saw man as a whole being responsible to himself, his community, and his government. To Parker, the point in analyzing the class structure of Boston, the moral condition of the city, and the conditions of poverty was to enlighten others to their duty as individuals and as citizens—to educate them to moral action. One of his substantial efforts to accomplish this education was the *Massachusetts Quarterly Review*.

V *Massachusetts Quarterly Review*

Though Emerson was quite satisfied to be finished with *The Dial* in 1844, he was talking about starting another journal with Parker, Channing, Sumner, Alcott, Thoreau, and others. Parker was chosen to edit it and especially sought help from Charles Sumner, but Sumner declined, because he thought the time not good for publishing another journal. In May, Parker "invited a *Troop of Reformers*" to his house to discuss the publication and he finally convinced Emerson to help and Elliot Cabot to be the business manager. In June, Parker was ready to announce publication; but, in August, he was still seeking Emerson's contribution. Emerson wrote "To the Public," the opening for the first issue—published while he was in Europe—but was surprised to see himself listed as an editor. It was his only contribution. The journal was Parker's, who called it *The Dial* with a beard to convey his opinion that the earlier publication had had many immature contributors.

Parker told Sumner that the purpose of the journal was to publish American ideas abroad and to awaken Americans by letting them know that they lived in the nineteenth century and that utopia must be achieved, not awaited. Another purpose was to prove that an independent journal could exist that was open to every stripe of liberal opinion. In planning the contents of the new journal, Parker made his own list of subjects: political, moral, theological, philosophical, and literary ones; even such topics as the "Condition of China," the "Progress of France since Revolution," and articles about five English poets.

Parker also listed the people he wished to write for the publication under three headings—"Certain and Valuable," "Valuable but not Certain," and "Certain but not Valuable." Among the first are Emerson, John Weiss, Cabot, William Henry Channing, and Samuel G. Howe, the second lists Joshua R. Giddings, John G. Palfrey, George Ripley, and Nathaniel Hawthorne; and the third is remarkable for the number of Transcendentalists, including Margaret Fuller, William Ellery Channing, the younger, and Henry Thoreau.[17] Though the magazine is now considered one related to Transcendentalism, Parker's purpose was not to make it another organ for such expression. Though it would be liberal, the emphasis would not be on literature, philosophy, or even theology.

To a large extent, the articles would be concerned with history and politics. The magazine shows more dramatically than Parker's letters and his journals his new interests—his new field of combat in this decade.

Parker, Emerson, and Weiss were the Transcendentalists who contributed to the *Massachusetts Quarterly Review.* (Others, such as Thomas Wentworth Higginson and John S. Dwight, may have written short notices.) A few of the contributors—including George Finlay, Edouard Desor, Samuel Brown—were not Americans. Americans who did contribute were the historian, Richard Hildreth, S. G. Howe, Henry James, Sr., and Samuel Ward—a diverse group of writers brought together by Theodore Parker. Most of the contributors were liberals, and many of them worked for the abolition of slavery—at least seven belonged to the Vigilance Committee of Boston. But Abolition was not the absorbing interest of the *Review;* for, if the publication did not have the freshness that one might expect, as George Ripley charged in a review in *The Harbinger,* it at least was not narrow. When it failed in 1850, a failure due more to the printer than to the editor or his contributors, the publication was not succeeded by any new periodical of its caliber. As Clarence Gohdes suggests, it was in a sense a father of the *Atlantic Monthly* which appeared in 1853 and which was founded by Francis H. Underwood, one of Parker's congregation, with the support of James R. Lowell, Parker, Hildreth, Howe, and Wendell Phillips.[18]

Parker's contributions to the *Review* reveal significant developments in his work. To the first issue he contributed "The Mexican War," a review essay of the President's message to a joint session of the Congress on December 8, 1846. Parker, who applied some of his methods of theological study to political affairs, began with a sketch of war as viewed by civilized and barbaric nations and by theorists, philosophers, economists, and philanthropists. He then focused on the Mexican War. Having moved from the general to the specific, a practice which has been noted as typical for him, he gave a detailed résumé of the events leading to the war and included many quotations from state papers. He reviewed the action of the prominent men in Congress—Thomas Hart Benton, John C. Calhoun, Henry Clay, and Daniel Webster—and concluded his fifty-page article with the charge that the real cause of the war was the slave power in the United States which controlled the federal government and its actions.[19]

In his continuing attempt to describe, define, and finally to improve the government, Parker had given a discourse on John Quincy Adams in March, 1848; and it was reprinted in the June, 1848, issue of the *Review*. Again using his customary method, Parker began with a rhetorical construct into which he placed his specific subject. This time it was the ranking of men as discoverers, organizers, and administrators; and Adams was at best an administrator. To evaluate him more generously, Parker found a key—Adams's devotion to freedom—which lead him to eulogize: "The slave has lost a champion who gained new ardor and new strength the longer he fought; America has lost a man who loved her with his heart; Religion has lost a supporter; Freedom an unfailing friend, and Mankind a noble vindicator of our unalienable rights." The piece is charitable and restrained. Though Parker found much to praise and little to damn, he could not find in Adams those qualities for which he was looking. He could not find him as worthy of his admiration as Benjamin Franklin.

In this article another quality of Parker is revealed. In describing his categories of men, he defined the discoverer of religion: he is one "who discovers an idea so central that all sectarianism of parties or of nations seems little in its light; who discover and teach the universal law which unifies the Race, binding man to man, and man to God; who discover the true method of Religion conducting to natural worship without limitation. to free Goodness, free Piety, free Thought." [20] Though nominally a description of a category and bearing little relation to Adams, it describes what Parker wished to be if not what he already saw himself as being. William Ellery Channing, who might have held Parker's highest esteem among the clergy, was described in an article a few months later in September, 1848, as "the most remarkable clergyman in America," but not as a discoverer. [21] He lacked originality and the impulse for reform, being too timid and cautious. Here again Parker hinted that another lacked the qualities he possessed, but there is no reason to suspect that these were conscious suggestions.

Two articles which reveal Parker's method of approaching the political situation appear in the December, 1848, issue. In "The Political Destination of America, and the Signs of the Times," Parker identified the unique quality of America as "LOVE OF FREEDOM; OF MAN'S NATURAL RIGHTS." The nation's task was "TO ORGANIZE THE RIGHTS OF MAN." He found among its chief characteristics "an Impatience of Authority," including precedence and tradition; "a Philosophic Tendency," searching for first, ultimate, and eternal principles though not yet finding them; "a great Intensity of Life and Purpose" (under this head he includes American literature which is best in "speeches, pamphlets, and newspapers"); and "Excessive Love of Material Things."[22] This and other articles of its sort are too impressionistic and general to have real substance, but they clearly reveal Parker's conception of his nation.

On the other hand, another article in the same issue, the substantial "The Free Soil Movement," contains a careful description of political parties in America. Parker tried to show how the Whigs and Democrats differed mainly on trade and finance while the new party concerned itself with the question of slavery in states and territories. Since, to Parker, this proper concern of political parties was overlooked by the major parties, he showed its importance:

Such was the state of things in 1831. Antislavery had "an obscure hole" for its head-quarters; the one agitator, who had filled the two doughty governors of Virginia and Georgia with uncomfortable forebodings, had "a negro boy" "for his only visible auxiliary," and none of the respectable men of Boston had heard of the hole, of the agitator, of the negro boy, or even of the agitation. One thing must be true,—either the man and the boy were pretty vigorous, or else there was a great Truth in that obscure hole; for in spite of the governors and the mayors, spite of the many able men in the South and the North, spite, also of the wealth and respectability of the whole land—it is a plain case that the abolitionists have shaken the nation, and their Idea is THE Idea of the time, and the party which shall warmly welcome that is destined before long to override all other parties.

Because Parker believed the people would support an antislavery party, his purpose was to urge Free Soilers and others to unite to form one Abolition party.[23] By 1848 he saw the necessity of concerted political action rather than scattered, individual attempts to change the minds of men, though he continued his own efforts in both ways.

The list of proposed subjects for the *Review* which Parker had written included most of his own interests, among them politics and history. Just as he as a reformer hoped to change the apparent course of the government, he also wished to alter the writing of history. Parker hoped to write a history of civilization, speaking of it repeatedly in his journal; and he was properly concerned, therefore, with the craft of the historian. Reviewing the works of William M. Prescott gave him the opportunity to present the theories he was developing. He defined the task of the historian as one dealing with every aspect of a nation and its people, as telling not only what had occurred but what ought to have been: "When all these things are told, History ceases to be a mere panorama of events having no unity but time and place; it becomes a Philosophy teaching by experience, and has a profound meaning and awakens a deep interest, while it tells the lessons of the Past for the warning of the Present and the edification of the Future." [24]

To Parker, Prescott was not a very good historian because he knew so little about the philosophy of history. He recounted the events but not the meaning or the causes, and he failed to place the events in the history of the race. Prescott was therefore, only an average man with an average conscience. In reviewing the Conquest of Mexico, Parker specified that Prescott failed to ask "what RIGHT had the Spaniards to invade Mexico and possess themselves of its soil." [25] Similarly, Prescott failed to judge the Spanish cruelties with sufficient severity. Parker wanted righteous history in which the historian would not only tell all, but judge all.

For the last volume of the Massachusetts Quarterly Review Parker wrote four articles. Doubtless he did not, at the beginning of the year, plan the four as a summary of his current interests and activities; perhaps, therefore, they only reflect his sense of balance in his work. In the order in which they appear, the four are: "Mr. Polk's Administration," "The Writings of R. W. Emerson," "Hildreth's History of the United States," and "Different Christologies of the New Testament."

"Mr. Polk's Administration" reveals Parker's continuing interest in the practical matters of statesmanship and in the problem of finding worthy leaders—a puzzle which absorbed him for the rest of his life. Parker could scarcely admire President Polk: "Mr. Polk was remarkable neither for thought nor action; he had no virtues or vices to distinguish him from the common run of politicians, who swim with the party tide, up or down, in or out, as it may be." So bland did he find Polk that he professed that only the "Ideas of the [Polk's] Administration" could be discussed. But Parker's subject was the administration, and he began with the conditions existing when Polk took office. So prosperous was the nation that Parker concludes; "It must be a very bad government which, in four years, can seriously injure a nation like this, where so little depends on the central power." Immediately and directly Parker then presented the facts of the Mexican War and soon the charge that "The President made the war. . . ."

Most of the article is concerned with the Mexican War, particularly with the statistics of troops, costs, and so forth. But at the end of the article Parker returned to the man who occupied the position of potential power, who "demonstrated . . . the folly of putting a little man into a great man's place; the folly of taking the mere creature of a party to be the President of a nation." Parker even declared this occasion to be the first, though not the last, on which such a president has been in office. Yet, appropriate to Parker's belief in the strength of the nation—that is, its people—he confessed that even Polk could not damage "the nation's march." He could not impede the nation because "We are a new people in a new world; flexible still and ready to take the impress of a great Idea. Shame on us that we choose such leaders; men with no noble gifts of leadership, no lofty ideas, no humane aims; men that defile the continent with brother's blood most wickedly poured out!" The people were good; the parties, bad. Polk was only a man of party.

The nation needs to fear only "two modes of irresponsible power": that of party and that of gold.[26] Though he had quite early recognized the dangers of plutocracy, Parker, as he became more aware of the importance of political parties, came to recognize their power: either party could control the government to the virtual exclusion of those outside. He could accept neither the Democrats or the Whigs in 1848 or thereafter, but at this time he was more prepared to look to the Whigs than to the Democrats for help.

Though often disappointed in the politicians and statesmen to whom he looked for leadership, Parker could yet find men worthy of his admiration—and one of these was Ralph Waldo Emerson. The portrait of Emerson and his ideas in the issue following that containing the article on Polk contrasts sharply and meaningfully with the view of the late President. Though even Parker did not expect to find an Emerson in the White House, he hoped to find such qualities there. Though he and Emerson were scarcely the best of friends, Parker in full sincerity presented Emerson with generosity and good will.

Among Emerson's important traits was his quality of being "the most American of writers." Parker meant that Emerson represented the ideas of America—freedom, dignity, self-reliance. He admired Emerson's adroitness in combining the knowledge of books with that of nature, though Parker rather too carefully pointed out his limited acquaintance with books—"Here is a man familiar with books, not with many, but the best books. . . ." And Parker admired Emerson's versatility, his scope, his refusal to be dominated by a single idea. The importance of religion and of man, of the will of man, of intuition rather than induction or deduction, are primary with him; but Emerson erred in deprecating long, hard study of books; argument; and discipline. These values were, after all, Parker's and his view of Emerson's judgment reveals more about Parker than about Emerson—as well as a deeper appreciation of Emerson's writings than of the man. To Parker, Emerson was cold and deficient in logic; again, Parker's own strength—at least as he saw himself—are emphasized.

Parker, who found fault with the organization of Emerson's essays, explained that individuality means so much to Emerson that order means little. Like many later critics, Parker praised in Emerson's writings axioms such as "It needs a divine man to exhibit anything divine" and "Every great man is unique." It was the line, the axiom, the aphorism which Parker liked in Emerson's writing rather than the essay. Although he regretted the lack of logic and the exaggeration of the importance of intuition in Emerson's writings, Parker extolled Emerson's "intellectual and moral sincerity," his lack of compromise, and his concern for "Truth, Justice, and Beauty." Emerson was a Christian with a passionate concern for mankind rather than for party, section, or church.[27] The righteous and self-conscious Parker revealed again, as he did in most of his best essays on men, his view of himself. Often in his writings Parker implied that others had the good qualities he himself possessed and that he did not share their shortcomings. He was seldom humble.

Reviewing Richard Hildreth's *History of the United States* gave Parker the opportunity to present his own opinions and theories of American history.[28] Though he finally discussed

Hildreth's work, most of the essay consists of his own views. He found a pattern in American history which was not the result of the efforts of men such as Captain Smith or Roger Williams: "Looked at carelessly, they [Georgia and New Hampshire] seem only divergent, but, when studied carefully, it seems as if there was a regular plan, and as if the whole was calculated to bring about the present result. No doubt, there was such a cancatenation of part with part, only the plan lay in God. . . ." America was, therefore, the culmination of one phase of God's plan; it was the place where "universal democracy" would first be exemplified. According to Parker, God's plan decreed that the man of Georgia—the secular man—would unite with the man of New Hampshire—the religious man—"to form a future national man, namely the Western man."

Parker saw two periods in history. The first was characterized in politics by the dominance of the state over the individual and in religion by ante-Christian forms. In the second came democracy, "the government of all, for all, and by all," and absolute religion, Parker's brand of Christianity. The settlement of America marked the turning point from the first to the second period. As the colonists came, "Virgin America, hidden away behind the Atlantic and Pacific oceans, is now to be married to mankind." Parker's view of history was theological and millennial; the movement of events, ideas, and institutions was not traceable to man's efforts or accidents but to God's plan. The modern reader who carefully reads the review may be puzzled by Parker's praise of Hildreth for writing objective history, but Parker also regarded his own interpretation as objective and his own view of history simply as truth.

In the final issue of the *Review*, as though to reveal that he had not forsaken his career of a scholarly theologian, Parker wrote "Some Thoughts on the Different Opinions in the New Testament Relative to the Personality of Jesus."[29] Rather a casual essay on the nature of Christ, this article presented in some detail the views of Christ found in the New Testament. Parker carefully concluded that "We thus see the gradual elevation of the personality of Christ, from the son of Joseph and Mary to the Son of God, with a distinct pre-existence before he 'was made flesh,' a God who was in the beginning, who made all things, is one with the Father, but still dependent on him, and inferior to him." Parker reached this conclusion after carefully tracing the descriptions of Christ through various books of the New Testament and did not attempt to generalize upon it or to leap to its application to absolute religion, to Unitarianism, or to Christianity. The article much resembles some of the work he had done for the *Scriptural Interpreter* fifteen years before.

The writing Parker did for the *Review* virtually marks the end of the period of his widest activity. Though the interests continued his time was to be more and more consumed by the work of antislavery—indeed, in a few years Parker was to be for many wholly identified with the antislavery cause. Though he did not forget or neglect his concern for poverty, crime, or incompetent leaders, he recognized that slavery stood in the way of the industrial democracy and of the earthly salvation he envisaged. Still he sought a leader, an Emerson—or a Parker—in a position of power; but he was not content, as were other Transcendentalists, merely to lament the inaction of others; Parker acted.

CHAPTER 5

The Abolitionist

S lavery, which slowly became the central problem for Parker, by 1850 finally absorbed most of his time and interest. In the early 1840's his ostensible concern was slavery in general and in the abstract, but soon his attention was directed wholly to Negro slavery in the Southern states. As he turned to the problems of stopping the expansion of slavery and of destroying the institution, he became more involved with political issues; for he realized that politics was the instrument through which righteousness would have to act. At the same time, he realized that people would have to be convinced of the wrong of slavery and of the justice of abolishing it. Parker therefore assumed two primary tasks: to convince his audiences of the evil of slavery through statistics, exhortation, and pleas for justice; and to persuade politicians to act on the basis of right. The passage in 1850 of the Fugitive Slave Law increased his ire and his activity because he felt that the North was thereby forcibly brought to support slavery. The rendition of slaves—sending them back to their masters—under that law was a touch of hell to Theodore Parker.

Behind all of Parker's actions to eliminate slavery was his belief in Christianity. His absolute religion, dictated not only that all men were created equal and that all men were brothers, but also that this nation was destined by God to become a utopian democracy. With slavery, this achievement was impossible. In his own view, Parker never deserted his position as the spokesman for absolute religion. He turned to antislavery activity to make the nation's conversion to righteousness possible. The publication of two theological works during this decade of most intense antislavery activity demonstrates that he did not wholly neglect theology to work for the abolition of slavery.

Parker's speech during the Anthony Burns affair of 1854 caused his arrest and trial, but the authorities had obviously taken advantage of this opportunity to attack Parker since this speech was no more treasonous or inflammatory than many others he had given. The attack on Parker backfired as it gave him the chance to answer his enemies. When they deprived him of presenting his defense in court, he published it as *The Trial of Theodore Parker for the Misdemeanor of a Speech in Faneuil Hall against Kidnapping; with the Defence* (1855). Even during the campaign of 1856 and in the arguments over disunion, Parker insisted that right rather than compromise and justice rather than expediency should prevail. To separate from the South would divorce the North from Negro slavery, but what would such action do for the slaves and for the poor whites? His view encompassed the nation which was the result of God's plan, not the political rearrangements which might result from man's meddling. The nation must be rid of slavery. To this end, Parker gave hundreds of lectures and sought the leader he never found to guide the nation. His actions were required by his religion— sufficient reason for Theodore Parker.

I   *Attacks on Slavery Before 1850*

Before 1848 Parker gave only one published sermon and few lectures on slavery, although he did refer to it in his social sermons of the decade. The first sermon on slavery was delivered in January, 1841, the same month in which he delivered the South Boston sermon, "The Transient and the Permanent in Christianity." These two sermons established the two major areas of reform he was to work in—theology and slavery; in them, he set forth the outlines of the arguments he would use; and, from them, Parker's notoriety sprang. In his "A Sermon of Slavery" he presented the arguments which he employed against that institution for the next twenty years.[1]

Characteristically, he began the sermons with definitions—in this sermon, of slavery, freedom, and man's state. "Now man was made to be free, to govern himself, to be his own master, to have no cause stand between him and God, which shall curtail his birthright of freedom." His argument was based on theological and political concepts of freedom and slavery. He further defined freedom as "a state in which man does, of his own consent, the best things he is capable of doing at that stage of his growth." This definition is a particularly appropriate one for a Transcendentalist who believed in the potential for growth—each man had the possibility of doing what he could with his own capacity for development, though the capacity itself was not a matter of free will. Though the sermon is nominally on bondage rather than on Negro slavery, Parker did not avoid the Negro's situation for long. He rejected arguments that asserted the reasonable conditions of the slaves and those that compared Southern slavery with the wage slavery of the North. And he refused to oppose the slaveholders on the ground that they were not Christians.

In this first sermon about slavery, Parker told one of his best illustrative fables. He imagined a race of men living at the bottom of the sea under a government and a religion which, not surprisingly, include all the abstract principles of American democracy and Protestantism. If one were told that in half of this land slaves were held, he would immediately declare the race hypocritical. Though the parable is obvious, its point was well made: Parker showed the relation of the North to the South with regard to slavery. The North bought Southern products, obviously associated with it politically, shared guilt by ignoring the crime, and neglected its duties as brother's keeper. The cause of slavery was "the desire to get gain, comfort, or luxury; to have power over matter, without working or paying the honest price of that gain, comfort, luxury, and power; it is the spirit which would knowingly and of set purpose injure another for the sake of gaining some benefit to yourself." Though Parker had to admit that such chattel or wage slavery also existed in the North, he did not here—or ever—deal at length with that problem.

Southerners charged that wage slavery in the North was at least as bad as Negro slavery in the South, and Parker's definition of the cause of slavery served for both types. But he could not admit that both were equally bad, for the industrial democracy which he anticipated would allow wage slavery though not human bondage. Had he been acutely concerned with converting a Southern audience, he could easily have distinguished between the two types of slavery; but whether or not he could have proved the Northern factory worker to be economically free is another question. Since, in his view, Southern slavery was legal and yet wrong, the law, even the Constitution, had to be changed; for the laws of men had to conform to those of God.

There was another sort of slavery which he touched upon from time to time through the sermon. At one point he called it "internal restrictions" to freedom, at another "soul-slavery." It was caused internally "by some passion or prejudice, superstition or sin." "Body slavery is so bad that the sun might be pardoned if it turned back, refusing to shine on such a sin; on a land contaminated with its stain. But soul-slavery, what shall we say of that?" He can say little more of its horrors. Parker tried to write of abstract slavery which included the slavery of the Negro in the South; but, if the attack on Negro slavery was weak, that on "soul-slavery" was so vague as to be entirely ineffective. Finding greed to be the cause of both and designating the latter as the more heinous weakens his attack on the former.

Though the sermon is important for the development of Parker's personal antislavery effort, it is remarkably weak as a rhetorical accomplishment. From it, one could conclude that slavery exists everywhere in many forms; and, since it is due to the greed of the individual, its elimination is as difficult as that of sin itself. Slavery would be removed when righteousness was attained. The writer is Parker the Transcendentalist rather than Parker the Abolitionist. The sermon belonged in *The Dial*, not on the Abolitionist platform.

A continuation of this course of abstraction and generalization is a speech delivered to the meeting of the American Anti-Slavery Society in celebration of the abolition of slavery by the French in April, 1848.[2] When Parker spoke of equal rights and universal suffrage, he noted that, though liberty and equality are American ideas, they have never been American facts. "America sought liberty only for the whites," he said. "Our fathers thought not of universal suffrage." His approach was again indirect: he did not attack Negro slavery in the United State frontally.

A few weeks later, when he addressed the New England Anti-Slavery Convention,[3] he began with the aim of the Abolitionists— "to remove and destroy the institution of slavery"—and their central ideas—that "all men are created free and equal which is the idea of Christianity, of human nature." However, as Parker pointed out, the thirty-one New Englanders in Congress, only five were even antislavery; since the Republic began, the presidency had been occupied only twelve years by men from the free states; Taylor, a Southerner and a general in the war against Mexico, was to be the nominee of the next Whig convention. Political action could destroy slavery, Parker noted; but the national parties must be convinced they can benefit from abolition. The

Abolitionists will finally succeed because they act with the "spirit of the age." Christianity and the rights of man, part of that spirit, will triumph against the practical atheism of their foes. This speech, especially its references to segregation in the Boston schools and its comments on the inclination of Anglo-Saxons to protest only for their own rights foreshadowed the Parker of the 1850's. His concern with political power is characteristic not only of his own work but of that of the New England conscience wing of the antislavery movement.

In the minds of Parker and other New Englanders, as the political power of the New England states, particularly of the New England aristocracy, declined, the power of the South grew. Slavery became more important to the South; the number of slaves increased. The rise of the South, the decline of New England, and the increase in slavery coincided. As these Easterners—consciously or unconsciously—saw it, New England could only regain power by eliminating slavery. The South could then be overcome by the North, and New England could again direct the power of the federal government and the course of the nation. Though most of Parker's addresses rest on this analysis, he did not explicitly connect Abolition with the recovery of power by the New England states. He did, however, believe in the moral superiority of the Abolitionists and in the inevitable elevation of the moral tone of the nation if New England did regain power.

Though Parker spoke at various antislavery meetings before 1848, his first lengthy published statement to the general public is *A Letter to the People of the United States Touching the Matter of Slavery*; and it marks a new phase in his antislavery work. Parker tried in this hundred-page pamphlet, as he did in the Levi Blodgett letter of 1840, to use a persona effectively. The speaker describes himself as "an obscure man," "one of the undistinguished million," who had "no name, no office, no rank" and is "no aspirant for office or for fame." He speaks because political and religious leaders have kept silent and because to speak is a matter of conscience and duty. Slavery touches him as it does all citizens because the nation supports it through legislation and war; through its extension into the Louisiana territory; through allowing slave markets even in the capital; through permitting no sanctuary for fugitives. He calls upon his fellow citizens because the politicians are busy with other things; the leaders will not admit to the evil. Because men must respond to slavery as human beings, he asks his audience to "decide and act according to Reason and Conscience."[4] With these words the persona is clearly dropped, and it is Parker who speaks.

In giving lengthy statistics on slavery and a history of the institution. Parker again used the devices of *A Sermon of War* (1846). He related the history of slavery to the Declaration of Independence, the Articles of Confederation, the Ordinance of 1787, and the Constitution. Having placed the institution in American history, he described the conditions of the slaves. He introduced the "Idea of Slavery," a phrase which he was to use again and again, often opposing it to the "Idea of Freedom." Much of the pamphlet concerned the effects of slavery on industry, population, education, law, and politics. Retarding industrialization was one of its effects. Only in the North did the invention of machines to replace manpower occur; in the South, no one wished to replace it. Parker assumed a value in industrialization which he did not specify.

Repeatedly, he supplied such statistics as these: "In 1839, the value of all the annual agricultural products of the South, as valued by the last census, was \$312,380,151; that of the free \$342,007,446." Using such figures, he proved that the population of the North had increased faster than that of the South and that the North had produced more poets, more scholarship, more books, more schools. When he compared New York and Virginia in detail, he blamed all the differences on slavery which necessitated a whole set of laws relating to slaves, their relations among themselves, to their masters, to the law itself. Its effect on politics had been to give the South disproportionate power in the Congress and in the presidency. Beyond all these effects, slavery was a sin—a crime against the Declaration and against humanity:

When you remember the intelligence of this age, its accumulated stores of Knowledge, Science, Art, and Wealth of Matter and of Mind, its Knowledge of Justice and eternal Right; when you consider that in political Ideas you stand the first people in the language of mankind, now moving towards new and peaceful conquests for the human race; when you reflect on the great doctrines of Universal Right set forth in so many forms amongst you by the senator and the school-boy; when you bring home to your bosoms the Religion whose sacred words are taught in that Bible, laid up in your churches, reverently kept in your courts of justice, carried under the folds of your flag over land and sea—that Bible, by millions multiplied and spread throughout the peopled world in every barbarous and stammering tongue,—and then remember that Slavery is here; that three million men are not by Christian Republican America held in bondage worse than Egyptian, hopeless as hell,—you must take this matter to heart, and confess that American slavery is the greatest, foulest Wrong which man ever did to man; the most hideous and detested Sin a nation has ever committed before the just, all-bounteous god—a Wrong and a Sin wholly without excuse.[5]

In concluding appeals of this sort, Parker always appealed to men's moral conscience in the broadest sense rather to narrower sectarian principles.

In his "Conclusion," addressed to "Fellow-Citizens of America," he spoke first of the effects and cost of slavery. He offered no easy solution. He came back to the state of the civilization of the world, its continual progress, and remarked, "America, the first of the foremost nations to proclaim Equality, and Human Rights inborn with all; the first confessedly to form a State on Nature's Law—America restores Barbarism; will still hold slaves." The nation which he called the "latest Hope of Mankind, the Heir of sixty centuries—the Bridegroom of the virgin West" had slavery, had barbarism. To all this greatness and potential came "the NEGRO SLAVE, bought, branded, beat."[6] So he closed—without a plea for action, without a plan for action, without exhortation really, but with a plea for civilized justice. Purity had been violated and must be restored. With astonishing clarity, Parker saw the real nation as the mythic nation. The metaphor *was* the reality. There was no nation but the Bridegroom. Such an image led to the necessity of removing sin, to the duty of perfecting the Hope of Mankind.

Parker's *Letter*, like much of his other work on slavery, reveals what he valued. Civilization, humanity, mankind—these abstractions he often placed on a level with Christianity; for the Christianity he preached as absolute religion includes them as virtues. The nation as the potential fulfillment of the promise of these abstractions had a sacred trust to be true to them. Progress was only a general label for the course of the nation which he conceived in terms of growth—population, wealth, industralization. Since slavery impeded such growth, Parker considered it a sin against Christian morality and against the nation entrusted with the divine mission. The missionary zeal of the Southerners who wished to control the government to preserve slavery, to extend slavery to the West, to the South, to the Caribbean and beyond, clashed directly with that of those who thought, as Parker did, of the mission of the North to extend its values to the West, to the South, perhaps to Canada and to Central America. Slavery interfered with his goal of an industrialized democracy progressing to an ill-defined goal of a millennial state. Slavery was the complete sin; no other was needed. This conviction drove Parker and many other reformers quite conscientiously to turn most of their efforts against it.

The influence of such a publication as the *Letter* is almost impossible to discover. One response it provoked was a letter from a Southerner, J. J. Flourney of Georgia. He had read the *Letter* and advised Parker that he would accomplish little unless he could prove his position with support from the Bible. Parker, who thought this easily done, replied with that support, commenting on and interpreting biblical passages. Flourney would have none of Parker's theology or his interpretation of the Bible. In the fourth letter of the exchange, Parker said that he would prefer an opponent with whom he could reason.[7] He thought Flourney a particularly obtuse man, but the short exchange might have taught Parker something of the nature of the opposition he never saw.

II   *The Fugitive Slave Law*

Parker's attempts to influence others to act against slavery increased sharply about 1850, the year that marked the passage of the Fugitive Slave Bill which carried Parker and other New Englanders into a decade of sustained activity. In Faneuil Hall on March 25, 1850, Parker responded to Webster's famous Seventh of March speech. In the last great debate involving Webster, Clay, and Calhoun, Webster began, "I wish to speak to-day, not as a Massachusetts man, nor as a Northern man, but as an American, and a member of the Senate of the United States." However sweet these words might have sounded to a man of compromise, to Parker and others who would have no compromise with slavery the speech had no sweetness. That Webster spoke for the nation and against secession did not move Parker, for Webster accused the Abolitionists of having done no good; and, most heinous crime of all, he supported the Fugitive Slave Bill which, he said, merely restated man's duty as previously expressed in the Constitution.

Speaking against the bill which put fugitive slave cases under federal jurisdiction and which reasserted the North's authority and obligation to return fugitive slaves to the South, Parker asked whether freedom or slavery should be extended. He admitted that geography did not limit slavery; it must be limited by law. Parker himself had already hidden fugitives from slavery, and he did not intend to stop: "Does Mr. Webster suppose that such a law could be executed in Boston? that the people of Massachusetts will ever return a single fugitive slave, under such an act as that?" Parker could not believe that such a law could be effective in Massachusetts. In supporting it, Webster must be making "a bid for the Presidency," an act and motive that can only be compared to those of Benedict Arnold. Concluding one of his sharpest attacks to this time, Parker said: "Follow the counsel of Mr. Webster—it [slavery] will end in fire and blood."[8] The hostility of the rhetoric reflects the indignation Parker felt at the prospect of being legally forced to return fugitive slaves. For him, New England had become part of the slave South with the passage of the Fugitive Slave Law.

At a speech two months later before the New England Anti-Slavery Convention, Parker viewed political parties as sources of evil and again compared Webster to Benedict Arnold. He found none of the political leaders and none of the major party factions ready to fight slavery. Despite the conflict between freedom and slavery, despite the rising power of slavery from the time of the Constitution through the Mexican War, the politicians refused to act against it. He spoke of four political parties—the "Government party," the Whig, the Democrat, and the Free Soil. The first cared only for inaction; the second, for protection and slavery (its Southern wing favored slavery and protection), and the Democrats, almost solely in the tariff. Though the Free Soil party opposed the extension of slavery, it did not regard slavery as a sin. The clergy was also to blame for the continued existence of slavery. In general the "Toryism of America" is responsible for slavery. Parker defines a Tory as "one who prefers the possessions and property of mankind to man himself, to reason and to justice."[9] In opposition to the Tories were those who did not wish slaves returned after jury trial, those who did not wish slavery extended, and those who wanted freedom for all men.

The tone of persecution is evident in these speeches. Parker thought that few agreed with him; the politicians, the press, the clergy, and the merchants did not oppose slavery; but it would be surprising only to discover Parker agreeing with the majority. In social and political issues, as in theological controversies, Parker chose the radical position. Yet he usually lamented the lack of support for his position, even when a substantial minority agreed with him, as it did on the slavery issue.

Though Parker sought a leader for the Abolition forces, the characteristics of the desired leader are not clear. He should discover political ideas, implement these ideas, and administer the institutions which result. Parker asked for genius and admitted that few if any political leaders exhibited that quality. For him the best Presidents had been Washington, Jefferson, and John Adams. The rest had accomplished surprisingly little. More important, to him, were William Ellery Channing, the opening of the Erie Canal, and the railroads of Massachusetts. "Mr. Cunard, in establishing his line of Atlantic steamers, did more for America than any President for five-and-twenty years." In contrast is a typical President such as Taylor: "No prudent man in Boston would hire a cook or a coachman with such inadequate recommendation as General Taylor had to prove his fitness for the place." [10] He was a harmless man and even perhaps a good one, and fortunately he did little harm, said Parker after Taylor's death.

In Parker's view the times called for men of genius, of morality, of conscience; but, instead, there were Taylors in the Presidency. The mass of people in the North and the "humbler clergy" were in the party of freedom; but the slaveholders, the wealthy of the North, and the politicians were in the party of the North; and the politicians were in the party of despotism. Boston had 140,000 people with "intelligence, activity, morality, order, comfort, and general welfare" such as no European city had; yet there was poverty, "unnatural wealth," sin, and sophistry. The South, however, had no virtues. [11] Given this moral and political situation, Parker's judgment was that enforcement of the Fugitive Slave Law should cause the Union to be dissolved by the North. The South, having nothing to lose, would not voluntarily leave the Union.

In a sermon given in November, 1850, Parker expected to disobey the Fugitive Slave Law, and he also anticipated that others would do so. Law by legislature and by statute is not the highest law. Just as men cannot make one and one equal a number other than two, so they cannot say the sun moves around the earth or make the false true or the true false. There are "laws of the human spirit" and justice, that which is "absolutely right." Conscience is the faculty which discovers the rules for moral conduct: "It is the function of conscience to discover to men the moral law of God." Man obeys his conscience because his duty is to keep God's law; therefore, the duty of men is to rescue the fugitive slaves.

Though Parker himself detested violence, he could commit it under certain circumstances: "The man who attacks me to reduce me to slavery, in that moment of attack alienates his right to life, and if I were the fugitive, and could escape in no other way, I would kill him with as little compunction as I would drive a mosquito from my face. It is high time this was said. What grasshoppers we are before the statute of men! What Goliaths against the law of God!"[12] Men disobeyed the laws of God without a quiver but were faithfully and piously subservient to the laws of men. Such a view led to the accusation of treason against Parker.

By the end of 1850, Parker was devoting much time to the Vigilance Committee and to other antislavery activities.[13] New Englanders of Parker's persuasion began to act in earnest after the passage of the hated law, and one of Parker's tasks was helping fugitives such as the Crafts who had come almost two years before to Boston. The light-skinned Ellen had escaped with her husband who had posed as her slave; and both had become members of Parker's congregation. When Hughes (or Hews) a jailer, arrived from Georgia and applied under the Fugitive Slave Law for the papers to have the Crafts seized, they were hidden. The Vigilance Committee was able to force Hughes to run from Boston.

Parker wrote even to President Fillmore about the Craft case, proclaiming his duty to his parishioners. In his letter he admits that he had married the Crafts, and that afterward he had given William Craft a sword and a Bible and had suggested that each had its appropriate use. Parker asked: "When the slave-hunters were here, suppose I had helped the man to escape out of their hands; suppose I had taken the woman to my own house, and sheltered her there till the storm had passed by: should *you* think I did a thing worthy of fine and imprisonment?"[14] Parker virtually told what he had done. He concluded that he and his fellows had to obey the laws of God, even if it meant submitting to the punishments of the law.

Though Parker was unable to bring before the American Unitarian Association this question of duty under the law, he did succeed in bringing the matter to discussion before a meeting of the Boston Ministerial Conference. Almost immediately interfering with the discussion was a statement attributed to Dr. Orville Dewey that he would send his own mother into slavery to preserve the Union. When the discussion finally turned from the Union to the question of obedience to law, Ezra S. Gannett—Parker's mentor when Parker edited the *Scriptural Interpreter* fifteen years earlier— spoke in favor of obeying all laws on the grounds that all law must be obeyed and that a violation of one could lead to violation of all. Furthermore, Gannett argued, without the Fugitive Slave Law and obedience to it, the Union could not be preserved. Parker's answer was that to disobey one law does not lead to the disobedience of all laws; men obey laws because they help men to obey God's laws. He told them that to perform his own duty he wrote his sermons with a pistol in his desk and a sword beside him in case he had to defend the members of his church. He thought non-resistance to be "nonsense." [15] The Boston Ministerial Association could not agree on the duty of ministers under the Fugitive Slave Law. However strongly they might have been impressed by Parker's arguments on their duties under God's laws, they could not escape their belief in the meaning and importance of man's laws. Neither did many of them believe so fervently in their intuition of God's laws.

The response of the Unitarian ministers to his assertions revived in Parker the feelings of persecution and rejection that he had had a decade ago. To Sumner, he wrote: "you must remember that I am probably the most unpopular man in the land, certainly the most hated of any one in it." However exaggerated, this distinction which almost pleased him had resulted from his sermons on theology as well as his Abolition work. Some months later he wrote to his old friend, Convers Francis: "Think of me, hated, shunned, hooted at; not thought worthy to be even a member of the Boston Association of Ministers or of the P.B.K. [Phi Beta Kappa]! . . . I have no *child*, and the worst reputation of any minister in all America." [16] Yet Parker gained solace from thinking that he had at least achieved notoriety—for part of his ambition was to have his name known.

By the summer of 1852 Parker was convinced that Franklin Pierce would be elected President in the fall. The Democrats would then work to divide California into two states—one slave, one free. They would also try to take more territory from Mexico, to make slave states out of New Mexico and Utah, and to annex Cuba—the chief object and the most popular. Most of his estimates of the slave power and of the intentions of Democrats in the 1850's were wrong. But he correctly predicted the coming war. He thought his enemies—they were innumerable—capable of conspiracy and immeasurable evil. Events had occurred which had convinced Parker of the low moral condition of the North; and one of these was the return of Thomas Sims, a slave, to the South.

III   *1851-1854—Antislavery and Theology*

On February 15, 1851, a fugitive slave named Shadrach who had been taken into custody for return to the South was rescued from the Boston Court House. A short time later, April 3, 1851, another fugitive, Thomas Sims, was taken into custody. Parker was among the first to try to delay Sim's return, though he was able to accomplish little. The Court House where Sims was kept was barracaded and iron chains were put around the building. Friday, the day after the capture, when Sims's case was heard before Commissioner George Ticknor Curtis, Sims was defended by Robert Rantoul, Charles G. Loring, and Samuel E. Sewall, who went before the state supreme court for a writ of habeas corpus which Chief Justice Shaw denied. When the Vigilance Committee held a meeting about the Sims case on the Common on Friday afternoon and in Tremont Temple in the evening, a thousand people attended the evening meeting; and troops patrolled the streets. On Monday, Richard Henry Dana and Rantoul came before Shaw again with petitions, which were again denied. An attempt was even made to have Sims arrested for having stabbed an officer when he was captured; if he were sent to prison for this crime, he could not be returned to Savannah.

When another meeting was held in Tremont Temple on Tuesday, Thomas Wentworth Higginson and others formed a plan to have Sims jump from his third-floor room onto a pile of mattresses below; but, when their intentions were learned, Sim's windows were barred. Thursday morning Charles Sumner and Sewall

petitioned Judge Peleg Sprague of the United States District Court
for a writ of habeas corpus; Thursday evening they were joined by
Dana in going before Judge Woodbury on a similar mission.
Curtis delivered his opinion on Friday morning; another appeal
was made that afternoon; but all petitions failed. About three
hundred guards took Sims to the waterfront at dawn to put him
on board the *Acorn* for his return to Savannah. Parker had
met with others to consider ways of rescuing Sims, but they
could find no way. The lawyers had made every reasonable
attempt to prevent Sims's return to Georgia and failed, while
those who counseled disobedience to the law were able to do
nothing. For the cotton Whigs of Boston, the rescue of Shadrach
had been avenged.

On the first anniversary of Sims's return to slavery where
Parker spoke before the Vigilance Committee at the Melodeon,
his subject encompassed what had occurred and what should
have been done. Parker rehearsed the facts of the Sims case,
though his audience must have known them well, and explained
that Sims was kidnapped because some men in Boston—rich
and respectable ones—wanted a fugitive returned to slavery from
their city. Not the people of rural Massachusetts or the middle-
class citizens of Boston but the wealthy were responsible. They
led Boston to desert its past and to discard the spirit of the Battle
of Lexington and the Revolution. While local government had
done nothing, the Committee of Vigilance had saved three or
four hundred "citizens of Boston" from being returned to the
South. The state should have opposed the desire of the wealthy
by passing a law making it a crime to kidnap a man in the fashion
permitted by the Fugitive Slave Law.

There is no paradox in Parker's advocating legal means to
save the escaped slaves. He was no anarchist; he wanted man's
law to reflect God's law; and only when it did not did he disobey
it. Additional evidence of his attitude toward the law is that he
supported most of the legal efforts to free Sims and later Anthony
Burns. On the occasion of the anniversary of Sims's return to
the South, when Parker dealt with the causes of the rendition
and the remedies that might have existed, he spoke as he hoped
an historian would: he presented the facts and judged them with
righteousness.[17]

Despite Parker's extensive involvement with the work of the
Vigilance Committee against slavery and for the fugitives who

came north, no fair account of this period of his life can be made without mentioning that in 1852 he published *Ten Sermons of Religion*, dedicating it to Emerson, and in 1853, *Sermons of Theism, Atheism and the Popular Theology*. Their publication came between the renditions of Sims and Burns, as though there had been some hiatus in his antislavery activity. The misleading coincidence might suggest that he left Abolition to return to theology. In fact, both volumes consist of sermons given over a period of time and, more important, serve as reminders that Parker regarded himself as a theologian whose religion dictated his duty to work for the elimination of slavery. Though it may be convenient to suggest that he forsook one field of endeavor to work in another, as most biographers have done, Parker never changed vocations. These two volumes, particularly the latter, contain the mature theology of Theodore Parker, though it must be added that neither containes new ideas never before presented in his sermons.

In *Sermons of Theism, Atheism and the Popular Theology* Parker attacked two poles of religious thought, atheism and the prevalent popular theology. Those who called Parker an atheist never read his sermons carefully enough to realize how profoundly he believed in a Deity. Although many orthodox clergymen could not admit it, Theodore Parker was as far from atheism as they themselves were. In the fifty pages devoted to speculative and practical atheism in this volume he proved in spirit and in fact how foreign atheism was to his religion. In brief, Parker did not believe one could be a speculative atheist (one who denies the existence of God); his belief in the religious faculty in every man precluded the possibility. Practical atheism (the denial of moral right, duty and obligation) he detested with all the strength a righteous man could muster.

Against the popular theology Parker marshaled another array of arguments including the truths he had found intuitively and those he had verified through the historical method of biblical criticism. As he had before, he attacked the conceptions of God and man and the relation between them in that theology charging that the popular theology viewed God as "the grimmest object in the universe," man as "a worm" and the relation between them as typified by the notion that God "loves one and rejects nine hundred and ninety-nine out of the thousand." Since he hoped his own absolute religion would displace popular theology,

he criticized it more harshly than he did atheism. The popular
theology was divorced from history, from reason, from conscience; it drove men from religion and separated science from
religion. He thought representatives of popular theology such as
Jonathan Edwards had driven more men from religion than
the famous atheists. Such theology was a religion of forms,
doctrines, and rituals without substance that easily permitted a
man to reserve his religion for a short time on Sundays.

Against atheism, popular theology, and Deism (which he would
never accept, though his enemies sometimes accused him of
accepting its doctrines), Parker set theism, the basis of absolute
religion. The keystone is God, who is "not so much a Being,
as a Becoming," perfect and infinite. "In nature God is the only
cause, the only providence, the only power; the law of nature
... represents the modes of action of God Himself, His thought
made visible. . . ."[18] Neither chance nor evil is possible in Nature.
There are no miracles and no providential occurrences, since nature
is perfectly ordered. Though God knows all that will happen in
history, He does grant man some freedom of will. Deriving his
religion from the absolute and ultimate source of all, Parker
named it absolute religion. Its thrust was to help all men to virtue
in fulfilling God's plan. Parker expected each man to act as he
himself did in working toward this end. Absolute religion provided
the impetus for man to act for piety and morality and against
drunkenness, crime, and slavery. Thus, Parker's theological writings
were a justification for his efforts against slavery.

Slavery was an issue which continued to absorb his time.
While the issue of organizing the territories of Kansas and
Nebraska was being discussed in Congress in 1854, he delivered
a sermon, "The Nebraska Question." His apparently circuitous
approach is his common technique of beginning with the general
and the abstract. He opened with "the general course of human
conduct in America" and attacked the Spanish for bringing greed
and the institutions of theocracy, monarchy, aristocracy and
despotocracy ("the dominion of the master over the exploitered
[sic] slave"). These caused the turn toward materialism which
has occurred generally in the country for "Wealth is the great
object of American desire. Covetousness is the American passion."
Money has been substituted for theocracy, monarchy, and aristocracy; and it has joined forces with despotocracy, as the
political parties have stood by and accepted the change. Now

the South wanted Nebraska. The South—"I must say it—is the enemy of the North." [19] She must be stopped, even at the price of Union. In Parker's lengthy attack on the South, he included his comparison of Virginia and New York and his catalogue of Southern triumphs. He found his theme and his facts, and he used them at every opportunity, fitting such issues as the Nebraska question into his view and approach.

But Parker seemed to some of his friends to have left religion and theology to work in other fields. When Senator Salmon P. Chase complained of this, Parker justified his own action in a letter to him. His first, and minor, point was that men would not favor slavery because of their prejudice against him; his theological position would not convert them to slavery. But his more important and more rational justification came from his view of the relation of slavery and theology. Parker based his position on his belief in growth principle, for he always opposed that which hindered the development of the individual and mankind.

If mankind were properly developed, the sins of slavery, war, and intemperance would not exist: "I became personally unpopular, *hated* even; but the *special measures* [antislavery] go forward obviously; the *general principle* enters into the public ear, the public mind, and does its work." [20] This concept was the heart of the matter for Parker: he preached a theology which asserted that man would improve as he recognized and accepted true principles. The sins against which he preached had to be removed in the course of development. Therefore, the removal of slavery was an application of his theology. When the idea of political morality became imbedded in the public mind, Parker would then help to organize men in order to achieve the ends dictated by the idea. First came the idea; then the action. This general approach permitted him to say with sincerity that it was slavery he opposed, not slaveholders. Since it was the institution that he attacked and studied, he subscribed to the *Richmond Examiner* and read as many other Southern publications as he could.

Continuing to reach for power and influence, Parker wrote to men in the government whom he thought might listen and be persuasive in the fight against slavery. To Seward he argued that freedom and slavery—North and South—were necessarily hostile to one another. There might be a separation, or freedom or slavery might win. The third alternative seemed most likely, in view of recent and predicted events. If slavery won, the nation would fall to despotism, and the nation "shall have committed the crime against nature, in our Titanic lust of wealth and power."[21] To stop this development, Parker proposed a convention of the Free States in Buffalo on July 4, 1854, "to consider the state of the Union." and to end slavery. A few days later he said in a letter to John P. Hale "If the South will not let it [slavery] down gradually, *we* must let *it down by the run.*"[22] The attempt to call a convention failed.

In speaking against slavery in 1854, Parker had these particular aims: to explain how it came to exist and to survive in the United States and to demonstrate why slavery had to be eliminated. He found the source of the North-South conflict in the types of people who settled the regions. Just as the differences between the settlers of North and South America created the differences between the countries of the continents, so the differences between settlers of North and South caused variations between the sections. The motivation of one group was religious and with it came democracy; that of the other was money or escape, and with it appeared oligarchy. Though the first sought theocracy, the people wanted democracy and achieved it; but they had not yet achieved perfection. For example, Negro children were still not allowed in the "common schools" because the Puritans did not reject slavery.

But the group which had settled the South had adopted slavery and had allowed the cruelties perpetrated within the system. The South, settled by those who wanted oligarchy, had been able to control the federal government: "It [the South] debases the legislative and the executive power; the Supreme Court is its venal prostitute. You remember the Inaugural of Mr. Pierce:— 'I believe that involuntary servitude is recognised by the Constitution. I believe that it stands like any other admitted right.'[23] To this statement of situation Parker compares what could be: democratic institutions and education can "give an intellectual development to the mass of men such as the world never saw." Men will be able to spend their time "subduing material Nature, and developing human Nature into its higher forms." Though materialism is now excessive, achievements will one day be in the realm of science, letters, and art.

IV   *The Rendition of Anthony Burns*

In the midst of these sermons and analytical addresses came another dark event which had serious consequences for Parker: the rendition of Anthony Burns.

For three years after the return of Sims, no fugitive slave was sent from Boston to the South, though as many as a thousand slaves escaped from their masters every year. Early in 1854 a group of Southerners had come to Massachusetts looking for three slaves and had discovered them in New Bedford; but, by the time they could get official help, the fugitives had disappeared; and the South was more than a little displeased. When Anthony Burns was arrested in Boston on May 24, 1854, he was taken immediately to jail and to a confrontation with his owner, Charles Suttle. Richard Henry Dana, Jr., the first man to learn of the arrest, rushed to help Burns. Though Burns refused his offers of aid, Dana was able to convince Edward G. Loring, the federal slave commissioner, to grant a two-day delay in the hearing.

The Vigilance Committee which met immediately, planned a large evening meeting. Thomas Wentworth Higginson prepared for action and bought a box of axes. That evening he was ready to supply axes to the mob that he expected to rush from the meeting. But those who were speaking at the meeting did not know of the plans of those who intended to storm the Court House. When the signal was given in the meeting, Parker, unaware of the arrangement, tried to calm the mob. Higginson, too impatient to wait for the dilatory mob from the meeting, stormed the Court House with only a few men. They battered down the door; Higginson was cut across the face; James Batchelder, a special policeman, was stabbed; and the would-be rescuers were forced to retreat. As a result of this action, Marshal Freeman wired Washington for instructions; President Pierce replied that the law had to be obeyed.

When Dana tried the various legal maneuvers which had been used in the Sims case, he succeeded in having the hearing delayed until Monday. On Saturday an attempt to gain Burns's release by purchasing him was stopped by District Attorney Hallett, who thought Washington and the South would be enraged if this purchase were allowed to happen, though Suttle had already accepted the $1200 offered him. During the three-day trial there was sufficient confusion in the evidence to warrant the release of Burns (faulty description and other technical errors), but Loring ordered him returned—a decision that did not close the matter in the minds of the people of Boston.

Sentiment had changed since 1851. The United States marshal had to rely upon "a precious set of murderers, thieves, bullies [and] blacklegs," according to Dana. To aid this unsavory group, troops were sent in from Rhode Island and New Hampshire; and over fifteen hundred Boston militia were on duty. As the troops moved Burns from the Court House to the waterfront past fifty thousand people, there was fighting; bricks were thrown at the soldiers; and men were beaten and sabered in return. But Burns was returned. A short time later, Louis Clark, a gambler and pimp who had organized the marshal's guard, hired "a drunken ex-prize fighter named Huxford" to attack Dana. Huxford hit him with an iron bar and left him bleeding and unconscious.[24] President Pierce paid over $14,000 to the mayor for the service of the State militia; the total cost for the rendition of Burns may have been over $100,000.

When Parker spoke in Fanueil Hall on Friday evening, May 26, in the midst of these events, he carefully asserted the right of the people to obey a law other than the slave law. He told his audience they could "put it [such obedience] into execution, just when you see fit." Only by implication did he suggest what they might do: "I love peace. But there is a means, and there is an end; Liberty is the end, and sometimes peace is not the means towards it." Such statements would cause his arrest and subsequent trial, though he did not urge the crowd to leave the hall to rush to the Court House. Later in his address, he even promised the crowd that it would not need to resort to arms to save Burns; he assured them that "if we stand up there resolutely, and declare that this man shall not go out of the city of Boston *without shooting a gun*—then he won't go back."[25]

Aware of the danger of exhorting his excited audience to action and thereafter being accused of treason, Parker in effect advised them to threaten and to show strength. If they did so, Burns would not be returned without battle; and Parker did not expect the guards to fight in order to return Burns to the South. If the city stood resolute, the authorities would retreat. The people almost followed Parker's advice; but the authorities, supported by the President and his power, were not so timid as Parker had supposed. As always, Parker overestimated the strategic plans of the South and underestimated the tactical acuity of the South and that of the federal government as its agent.

In one of Parker's sermons just after the rendition of Burns, *The New Crime Against Humanity,* Parker announced: "...there has been a man stolen in this city of our fathers." Though he knew everyone in his audience was familiar with the general facts of the case, he begins with these, admitting that he had played a central part in the affair and frankly estimating the importance of his message: "I know well the responsibility of the place I occupy this morning. To-morrow's sun shall carry my words to all America. They will be read on both sides of the continent. They will cross the ocean." The cause of the rendition under the Fugitive Slave Law was, to Parker, the battle between slavery and freedom. So strong was the control of the nation by the forces of slavery that, when Parker sent one of the three hundred petitions he had received for the repeal of the law to Eliot, the congressional representative from Boston, Eliot sent it back. Another official ridiculed was Edward G. Loring, slave commissioner, whom Parker pictured as coming to another court where he was asked, "Edward, where is thy brother Anthony?"; and Edward answered, "I know not, am I my brother's keeper, Lord?"[26]

The basis on which Parker continued to oppose the Fugitive Slave Law and to urge its repeal and disobedience to it was justice above law. Man must by will obey God's laws just as the falling leaf obeys natural laws. Parker admitted that there were laws which were not related to morality—voting age, interest, highway laws; but when a statutory law conflicted with justice, a situation discovered by conscience, justice must prevail. If, he said, a convention of murderers made murder legal, men obviously would not accept such a law since it would conflict with justice. The clash between justice and legislative law could occur whenever men did not look to their consciences. In arguing this principle of the supremacy of God's law, Parker did not always mention the Fugitive Slave Law; but this law precipitated the attack.[27] Parker, like most of his fellow Transcendentalists, did not explore the problem of conflicts among the consciences of men since he did not recognize the possibility.

Since Parker could never concentrate on a single problem, the summer of 1854, despite the significant Burns case, marked the occasion of other sermons on general problems such as "Dangers Which Threaten the Rights of Man in America." For Parker, the four most serious dangers were those from the "Devotion to Riches"; from the Catholic Church; from the idea that statute law was the highest law; and from slavery, which was based on that atheistic concept. These dangers stood in the way of the establishment of an industrial democracy. America was ruled by men with nothing but money and what it brought—by three hundred thousand slaveholders and their servants, North and South. So attractive was wealth that many Northerners turned from politics, military affairs, and all else to commerce and industry, though in the South the "ablest men almost exclusively attend to politics." Everyone attended to his financial interests. (Parker did not show how the industrial democracy could be built if men did not turn from politics.) The Catholic Church stood in the way because it opposed all that fostered democracy and the natural rights of man; it hated free churches, free press, and free schools; and its allegiance was to Rome. But Parker denied that he wished the Catholic Church excluded; for, if it could defeat Protestantism, "we deserve defeat."[28] The third danger, the prevalence of statute law, was countermanded by the examples of Christ, Luther, and the Puritans. If obedience to man's law were the highest virtue, what must be said of these "criminals."

The sum of these dangers was slavery. Parker saw three alternatives to resolve the conflict between slavery and freedom: (1) separation into two nations; (2) freedom destroying slavery; (3) slavery overwhelming freedom. He judged severance of the nation to be the most likely result; it would break up because of its large size and the general distaste for strong central government. But commercial interests and politicians benefited too greatly from the union to let it disintegrate soon. In the meantime, slavery would continue to conquer freedom, acquiring Haiti and Cuba, establishing slavery in all states, restoring the slave trade, and taking more territory from Mexico.

These dangers, including slavery itself, could be removed if men would recognize that the rights of man must prevail over the rights of property—and that religion must not be divorced from politics. The seeming simplicity of Parker's view of the national problems and their solutions is in large part a result of his efforts to make these clear to his audience. When reduced

entr鋼

to their simplest terms, his analyses are less convincing than
they appear in the vigor of his full presentations. Nevertheless,
Theodore Parker himself possessed such a compelling sense of
duty to right and to justice that he often cut through the complexi-
ties of national conditions and institutions in a fashion that
less confident men could not.

V *Parker's "Defence"*

Through 1854, a year in which Parker gave many addresses and
sermons, he anxiously awaited his own fate in the courts. There
had been an attempt to indict him for his part in the Burns
affair, though he did not believe it would succeed. In June his
enemies failed, but in October a true bill was brought in. In
December, Wendell Phillips was arrested; and the trial of both
Parker and Phillips was set for March, 1855. Parker feared
that the indictment would finally be dismissed and that he would be
cheated out of giving the defense which he laboriously produced.
When he was denied the opportunity to speak in court, he published his 221-page defense. Parker claimed this defense as his
first in fourteen years of being attacked. (In fact, most of his work
was a defense of his positions.) He now spoke because the right
of free speech was at stake. But first he felt compelled to outline
the circumstances leading him to publish his defense: "When
Judge Curtis delivered his charge to the Grand-Jury, June 7th,
1854, I made ready for trial, and in three or four days my line
of defence was marked out—the fortifications sketched, the
place of the batteries determined; I began to collect arms, and
was soon ready for his attack."

Like Parker's grandfather at Lexington, he readied his defenses.
Yet he was certain that Judges Sprague and Curtis "who have
taken such pains to establish slavery in Massachusetts," who
sat there "each like a travestied Prometheus, chained up in a
silk gown because they had brought to earth fire from the quarter
opposite to Heaven," would not allow him publicly to defend
himself. They would dismiss the indictment and put the blame
on the attorney for drawing a faulty bill. When the trial opened
on April 3, his lawyers "rent the indictment into many pieces."

Parker continued his review of the events: on June 7, Curtis
charged the grand jury looking into the Burns affair that "ob-
structing legal process of the United States is to be inquired of
and treated by you as a misdemeanor." Judge Curtis instructed

the jurors that such obstruction need not consist of violence; that, if a peaceable multitude should stop an officer without violence, this act was such obstruction. Not only were those who actually obstruct or oppose guilty, but those "leagued in the common design" and able to assist and those who "though absent when the offence [the attempted rescue] was committed, did procure, counsel, command, or abet others to commit the offence, are indictable." Moreover, those who advised obstruction were also indictable. Curtis informed the jury that it was not the place of men to decide which laws they would obey and which they would not, that local opinions about the extradition of fugitives were the road to mob rule. The grand jury did not return a true bill.

On October 16, another jury was impaneled. This jury brought in a true bill against Parker charging that he "then and there well knowing the premises, with force and arms did knowingly and wilfully obstruct, resist, and oppose the said Marshal Watson Freeman . . . in serving and attempting to serve and execute the said warrant and legal process . . . to the great damage of the said Watson Freeman, to the great hindrance and obstruction of Justice, to the evil example of all others, in like case offending, against the peace and dignity of the said United States, and contrary to the form of the Statute in such case made and provided." Indictments were returned against Phillips, Higginson, and others. Parker, who was arraigned on November 29 and released on $1500 bail, was to appear in court on March 5 and trial was fixed for April 3. The first motion that the indictment be dismissed was denied. Eventually a motion of *nolle prosequi* was entered, and the indictments were annulled.

In the opening of the defense itself, Parker described it as "more didactic than rhetorical, more like a lecture, less like a speech"; and so it is. He interpreted the charge for the jury: that his trial was a "Political Trial" and that he was charged with no act of self-ambition. He was on trial for his "love of Justice," for his "manly virtue." He presented himself as a minister who had been chiefly concerned with the "Laws of God" in studying "absolute, universal truth, teaching it to men, and applying it to the various departments of life."

Much of his *Defence* consists of his remarks on the situation in America, particularly "the Encroachments of a Power hostile to Democratic Institutions" and its attempts at the "Systematic

Corruption of the Judiciary" and of the right of trial by jury. Always he related his own trial to these larger topics: "I am on trial because I hate Slavery, because I love freedom for the black man, and for all the human Race. I am not arraigned because I have violated the statute on which the indictment is framed—no child could think it—but because I am an advocate of Freedom, because my Word, my Thoughts, my Feelings, my Actions, nay, all my life, my very Existence itself, are a protest against Slavery. Despotism cannot happily advance unless I am silenced."

Parker included almost fifty pages on the corruption of the judiciary, beginning with the judges under James I, "the first King of New England." It would be idle to rehearse even a part of this long discourse, and one wonders how Parker expected a jury to react to such a treatise. In addition to supplying historical data, he virtually gave a charge to the jury, explaining to it its function with respect to questions of fact, law, and the application of law to fact. After sixty pages of instructing the jury and telling it what and how it must decide, Parker moved to the general circumstances of his own case which occupy the remaining hundred pages of the defense. He supplied a history of the Fugitive Slave Law and its legal predecessors, its relation to the Constitution, and the cases which had arisen under it in Boston. He even attacked the judge and his family: "This family, though possessing many good qualities, has had a remarkably close and intimate connection with all, or most, of the recent cases of kidnapping [of slaves] in Boston."

Parker asked the jury, contrary to the judge's instructions, to consider the Constitution and the Fugitive Slave Law: "To me, it is very plain that kidnapping a man in Boston and making him a slave, is not the way to form a more perfect Union, establish Justice, insure domestic Tranquility, provide for the Common Defence, promote the General Welfare, or secure the Blessings of Liberty." In his long summary, Parker recounted that he had talked about the slave power and its plans, despotism in England, the corruption of judges, the perversion of trial by jury through the centuries, the course of slavery and slave power in America, and the Curtis family ("When Mr. Webster prostituted himself to the Slave Power this family went out and pimped for him in the streets. . . ."). Parker told the jury that it was deciding whether or not slavery would spread farther. As he closed, he

joined patriotism and religion, related John Hancock and John
Q. Adams to Moses and Aaron, and identified himself in the
courtroom with his grandfather at Lexington.[29]

The remarkable document which Parker called a "defence"
provoked little response. Originally directed at an audience of
jurors which could never have followed the elaborate arguments
and never have listened alertly to all two hundred pages of it,
the defense shares the characteristics of other Parker speeches.
From concrete situations and problems, the argument moved
toward historical background and abstract principles. Though
appropriate to treatises and discussion, such methods are often
not effective as arguments. The sections of the *Defence* presenting
the specific facts of the trial are the most persuasive. When Parker
presented his treatise on judges, jurors, and the judicial system,
he provided the "jury" with far more than it needed or could
digest. Despite his acumen for political affairs and antislavery
work, Parker's scholarly ambitions, ability, and knowledge continually interfered. Seldom could he achieve an appropriate relation between his work and knowledge as scholar and his effort
as a politician. Quite capable of arguing theological questions,
on the one hand, and the causes of a political situation, on the
other, Parker yet had great difficulty in gauging an audience.

In the midst of Parker's consuming antislavery activity, his
letters to Convers Francis continued with such information as
this: "I got from a foreign catalogue a copy of a rare book; *you*
doubtless know it well, but *I* never saw it before, though I have
been hunting for it some years: 'Epigrammata Clarissimi Dis-
sertissimique viri Thomae Mori Brittani pleraque ex Graecis
versa (Basilaea, apud Joannem Frobenium, Mense Martio, An.
MDXVIII)'."[30] Active as he was in public matters, Parker never
forgot the scholarly life he wished to pursue; but he could not be
both a secluded scholar and an active Abolitionist.

VI   *1856-58—Politics and Lectures*

Particularly as the 1856 elections approached, Parker renewed
his attempts to influence political leaders. To Governor N. P.
Banks he described the dichotomy between slavery and freedom,
arguing that the slave party had money, organization, and position;
but the freedom group had little of these though it did possess
ideas, genius, and "womanly women." He put it to Banks that, as

governor, he must want the party of freedom to have political power to carry out ideas: "How shall we do it? that is the question." (Shifts from "you" to "we" are common in Parker's letters.)

The things to consider were "the maximum of the new ideas which the people will accept in the next presidential election" and the minimum which they would accept. The minimum was a man who was so highly principled that the people could put their trust in him and in an appropriate platform for him. Chase had slipped by declaring slavery in the present geographic areas to be untouchable; Sumner, by his slogan "Freedom national and Slavery sectional." Parker could accept no slavery anywhere in the nation. The maximum acceptable to the people was the Declaration—all men are created equal with inalienable rights. The whole people would not yet accept this ideal, but it should be the goal. In the meantime, however, the North wanted the abolition of slavery and, indeed, would accept nothing less. Feigning innocence, Parker asked Banks if John C. Frémont, was a suitable candidate.[31] Though Parker felt he was not, he had to convince others.

Though Parker worked hard to find a suitable Presidential candidate, he had none to suggest. At the same time, he worked for the passage of a personal liberty law and in other ways to defeat and oppose the Fugitive Slave Law. He pressed Sumner to rouse the North, not because Sumner was the best man to do so but because Parker knew few others. War had begun in Kansas and in the Congress. An early stage could, Parker thought, become a Northern victory with a successful candidate in 1856. To be successful, the candidate needed the backing of conscience Whigs, errant Democrats, Northern Know-Nothings, Republicans, and antislavery party men. By the middle of April Parker had given eighty-four lectures in the previous four and a half months—and has done so while preaching weekly sermons, attending meetings, and writing over a thousand letters. Yet he said he had written only necessary notes.

Part of Parker's work in preparation for the election was the preaching of three of his best analyses of the conflict. Two of these, given on the same day, were published as *The Great Battle Between Slavery and Freedom*. The first, "The Present Aspect of the Anti-Slavery Enterprise," is primarily a description of the forces of slavery and freedom. That the antislavery forces were not working for the Negro as much as for the white man was made

clear by Parker who also said that, if Anglo-Saxons were enslaved,
they would fight for their freedom; but the Negroes were not
fighting.[32]

In the second sermon of the day, "The Present Crisis in
American Affairs," Parker established his view of the races. The
Caucasian had developed farthest and fastest to gain "power
over the material world." Of the groups within this most progressive race, the Teutonic led the way. Of them the Anglo-
Saxons, "or that portion thereof settled in the Northern States
of America, have got the farthest forward in certain important
forms of welfare, and now advance the most rapidly in their
general progress." Such descriptions of peoples and races can
only be made by men who have righteous conceptions of racial
and national character. Though Parker realized full well the
diverse parties and sentiments of the North, for example, he often
described the section without any recognition of the disagreements
within it. In this sermon he characterized the North as antislavery,
Christian, and industrial.

Viewing the nation as Parker did—with two opposing socio-
economic systems—it is no wonder he was ready for separation,
though he did not then advocate secession or disunion: "I do not
propose disunion—at present. I would never leave the black man
in bondage, or the whites subject to the slaveholding Oligarchy
which rules them." Furthermore, if the nation remained whole
and elected an antislavery man as President, federal offices could
be filled with antislavery men; Kansas and other new states would
be free; slavery could be restricted; a railroad to the Pacific built;
and the slave states would be surrounded by free states.[33] While
Parker perhaps expected too much of an antislavery President,
he did not overestimate the power of political force.

In the last of the three important published sermons of the
month, *A New Lesson for the Day,* Parker suggested that the
United States was in a "state of incipient civil war." The cases of
the Crafts, Shadrach, Sims, Burns, followed by the caning of
Sumner by Preston Brooks in the Senate, proved this assertion.
To convince his audience, Parker imagined Brooks as the representative of the South, Sumner of the North, so that the
blows fell on the members of his audience. In this presentation,
Brooks approached Sumner and stole "up behind him as he sits
writing, when his arms are pinioned in his heavy chair and his
other limbs are under the desk, and on his naked head strikes
him with a club loaded with lead, until he falls, stunning and

bleeding to the floor, and then continues his blows."[34] Parker
felt the impact of this attack both as an Abolitionist and as a
personal friend of Sumner. It increased his enmity toward the
South as the preserver of sin in the nation and provoked him to
work even more vigorously against the section and its evil.

Parker accepted Frémont's nomination, though he was far
from being his first choice; and through the summer he believed
Fremont could be elected. Yet he was convinced that, if Buchanan
were elected, there would be separation. Parker continued to
lecture frequently—over one hundred times between October and
August, 1856. He feared revolution and expected civil war; and,
though he could not go to Kansas, he followed events closely,
seeing the fight there as one between slavery and freedom. By
October, he saw defeat for Fremont and consequent civil war
within four years. He stopped buying books—he had spent
fifteen hundred dollars in a year for such purchases—to save
money for his wife. When war came, he thought his property
would be confiscated and himself hanged. Seldom had he been
so pessimistic, as he continued to believe in the coming war
between North and South and in an attempt by the nation to
conquer Cuba and then Mexico. Now he was not sure conditions
would have been better under Fremont; he doubted both the
man and the party, especially the Western Republicans. Though
Parker usually had more faith in the potential power of political
force than most Transcendentalists had, he occasionally shared
their distrust in the efficacy of institutions to improve men.

Despite the defeat of Fremont and Parker's subsequent depression, he would not attend the Disunion Convention that
Higginson and others called for January, 1857, on the grounds
that the recent election meant four more years of pro-slavery
government and an increasing hostility between the North and
the South. They believed the present union to be a failure and
called the convention "to consider the practicability, probability,
and expediency, of a separation."[35] When Parker wrote to Higginson the day before the convention to express his regret that other
business would keep him away, he approved the purpose of the
meeting though he did not favor separation since he continued
to believe it wrong to leave four million poor whites and four
million slaves under that government. But Parker had little faith
in the force of his argument, for in the last part of the letter he
suggested where the line between North and South should be
drawn. The land of freedom should be that east of Chesapeake

Bay, north of the Potomac and the Ohio, and west of the Mississippi. He thought Virginia and Kentucky might "beg" to stay
with the North. Like most other Abolitionists, Parker often mis-
judged the South.

Rather than sanction disunion, Parker continued to work for
Abolition under union. He lectured as often as he could, though
he knew the work was ruining his health. He believed in the value
of his work, considering the institution of the lecture as church,
college, and theater in one. He was certain the lecturing—"six or
eight of the most progressive and powerful minds in America
have been lecturing fifty or a hundred times in the year"—would
influence the people for the better.[36]

To understand the conditions of travel and the labor of lecturing
to a man such as Parker, who had also numerous responsibilities
at home, one may read his own accounts of such trips:

I gave up the Anti-Slavery Festival for the lecture, rode fifty-six miles in
the cars, leaving Boston at half-past four o'clock, and reaching the end
of the railroad at half-past six—drove seven miles in a sleigh, and reached
the house of ———, who had engaged me to come. It was time to begin;
I lectured one hour and three quarters, and returned to the house. Was
offered no supper before the lecture, and none after, till the chaise came
to the door to take me back again to the railroad station, seven miles
off, where I was to pass the night and take the cars at half-past six next
morning.

Luckily, I always carry a few little creature-comforts in my wallet. I ate
a seed-cake or two, and a fig with lumps of sugar. We reached the tavern
at eleven, could get nothing to eat at that hour, and, as it was a temperance
house, not a glass of ale, which is a good night-cap. It took three quarters
of an hour to thaw out:—went to bed at twelve in a cold room, was called
up at five, had what is universal, a tough steak, sour bread, and potatoes
swimming in fat. . . .

This experience was not unique, for one may read another account
from a letter to Sarah Hunt, written in 1857:

Monday last at seven, George and I walked down to the Lowell Depot,
and at eight started for Rouse's Point, two hundred and eighty-seven miles
off, sick and only fit to lie on a sofa, and have day-dreams of you, sweet
absent ones! and think over again the friendly endearments that are past,
but may yet return. A dreadful hard ride ends at nine P. M., and I find
myself in the worst tavern (pretending to decency) in the Northern States.
Bread which defies eating, crockery which sticks to your hands, fried fish

as cold as when drawn from the lake. Rise at half-past four, breakfast (?) at five, off in the cars at half past five, lecture at Malone that night, lie all day on the sofa, ditto at Potsdam next day.

The third day, leave Potsdam at nine, and reach Champlain (if I get there) at half-past eight, spending ten and a half hours in travelling by railroad ninety-three miles! Thence, after lecture, to Rouse's Point, and at half-past five to-morrow morning return to the cars which are to take me home.[37]

These tales of traveling through comfortable and civilized New England could have been told by most of the popular lecturers. Despite the difficulties of this work, Parker lectured to spread his views and to earn money for books and for antislavery work. So dependent was he on this income that the financial crisis of 1857 which caused the cancellation of lectures cut his income in half. Parker had lectured seventy-three times in the season by February, 1858. The previous year he had lectured eighty times "from the Mississippi to the Penobscot" in addition to his temperance and antislavery speeches.

The election of 1856 shows Parker's engrossment in practical politics on a national level. The next few years are punctuated by comments on politics and the Presidency. In 1858 he stated categorically that "Slavery must be put down politically, or else militarily." He asked for a Republican candidate in 1860 other than Frémont or some "Johnny Raw." He must be "a man who can wisely and bravely embody what public opinion there is already. Such a man is one of the forces that *make* public opinion." The President must not be "a fanatic, a dreamer, an enthusiast, but we don't want a coward or a trimmer." A man with these qualities could have been elected in 1856, but Fremont could not because he could not gain the trust of the people. Even the victory of the Republican candidate would not cause the South to leave the Union because it lacked industry, commerce, schools, and a sufficient population. He explained its threatening attitude in this way:

"Mamma," said a spoiled boy to a mother of ten other and older children, "Mamma, I want a piece of pickled elephant." "No, my dear, he can't have it. Johnny must be a good boy." "No, I won't be a good boy. I don't want to be good. I want a piece of pickled elephant." "But aint he mother's *youngest* boy? When we have some pickled elephant, he shall have the biggest piece!" "Ma'am, I don't want a *piece!* I want a *whole pickled elephant!* I want him *now!* If you don't let me have him now, I'll run right off and catch the measles. I know a boy that's got 'em first rate." [38]

But the South did leave the Union. Parker had underestimated the South in this respect, but he did not miscalculate its political strength and its tenacious fidelity to the institution of slavery. Why the South might want to keep its slaves he did not inquire; but, had he done so, Parker would have explained the reason in terms of the oligarchial greed for power.

There were continuing letters to William Herndon in 1858. In August, Parker wrote that he followed the Illinois campaign with interest and read the speeches—"the noble speeches"—of Abraham Lincoln; and he maintained his opinion that Stephen Douglas was a "mad dog." Though Parker favored neither Horace Greeley nor William Seward, he thought the latter would be the Republican candidate in 1860 to defeat Douglas. He told Herndon the battle was still between slavery and freedom, despotism and democracy. He hoped Lincoln would win, but he has just read the *Tribune* report of the Lincoln-Douglas debate at Ottawa and thinks Douglas had the better of it. Douglas had asked Lincoln the right questions on slavery, and Lincoln had dodged them. To Parker, "That is not the way to fight the battle of freedom." Worse, he said, "Daniel Webster stood on higher anti-slavery ground than Abraham Lincoln now." [39] Though Parker did not then realize it, Lincoln would almost wholly meet his prescription for a Republican candidate in 1860.

By this time, 1858, Parker occasionally could look back on the course of his career. When he had moved to Boston, he had thought of working among "the perishing class"—the lower class. But he discovered that people had "a great horror" of him; that men had no principles, "no correct ideas as a basis of action"; and that the slavery seemed so altogether such a crucial matter that it had to be dealt with first. [40] So Parker had spent his Boston years in setting forth his ideas on the proper relations between God and man and in fighting for Abolition. He was unable to deal with the lower classes, and he could not find men with principles; he could, however, work with a problem which he found significant on both a practical and an idealistic level. Parker must have realized the recurrence of the same difficulties he had as a teacher—being able to reach his pupils.

CHAPTER 6

The Closing Years

P arker preached some of his finest sermons in the closing
    years of his life, 1858 to 1860. Despite the pressure of varied
work, he was able to write sermons in his best direct style. Some
of these sermons summarize two decades of thinking and preaching; they come as part of a virtual capstone to this thought and his
battles with his theological enemies. So neatly do they round out
his life that it is quite difficult to imagine what direction he might
have taken after 1860 and particularly after the Civil War.
Furthermore, these sermons, coupled with statements in his letters
and in his journals, reveal his own expectation that his work was
drawing to a close. He was able to state clearly and succinctly
the theology he had preached, the theology by which he lived.

I *Sermons*

In one of these sermons, given February 14, 1858, "False and
True Theology,"[1] Parker approached his definition of theology
through an analysis of man's religious development which involves
emotions, ideas, and action—a three-part analysis which he earlier
had employed to describe the necessary steps in moving men
toward abolition. Theology proceeded from the middle term; it
was "The sum of ideas in religious matters. . . ." The ideas about
man, God, and the relations between them did not form merely
an academic body of thought but a science "whereof religion is
the practice." Since theology was the base for religion, it bore
directly on piety and morality.

Parker thus succeeded in drawing theology out of the study
and the divinity schools and putting it in the realm of men's
attitudes and actions. While in his younger days, he wished to
avoid the public life so that he could study theology; now he

argued that relations between theology, religion, and morality were so close that one could not separate theology from a life of principle: "As the theology which is accepted has such an immense influence on the individual, the community, the nation, or the race which accepts it, you see how important it is to have a right method in theology." After all, the "highest end of life . . . [is] to build up a religious character. . . ."

The false method in theology he called the "ecclesiastical method"; the true, the "philosophical method." In the false method, that accepted by most Christian sects, men assumed the authority of the Bible and deduced from it the doctrines to be believed. From this method came the existence of the devil, the depravity of men, the wrath of God, hell and eternal damnation, the Trinity and the divinity of Christ, the atonement of Christ, and the salvation through faith. These doctrines and the method which produced them Parker rejected. The conceptions of man and of God embodied in them he could not accept.

The true method rested on the assumption of the accuracy of the human faculties, including the religious faculty, and of the existence of the present world. The theologian who followed this method recognized both history and man's nature. He arrived at "a true theology, which shall be to the actual facts of God's nature, man's nature, and the relation between them, what astronomy is to the facts of the solar system. The science of theology will then be based on facts of observation and of consciousness, not on mere words. . . ." The false method in science resulted in astrology; in politics, in despotism. The true method in science gave astronomy; in politics, industrial democracy. The true method in theology "marries the religious instinct to philosophical reflection." Parker saw the discovery of its true and proper method as his contribution to theology. The method rests on the non-Lockean notions of perception that he had first accepted years before as he had entered the controversy with the Unitarians over miracles and inspiration.

In one of two sermons, given a short time later, on revivals in religion, Parker summarized the fruits of the false method in theology as false conceptions of God and of man leading to a false conception of religion, one which "is to save men from hell, and it is fit only for that."[2] The two sermons concerned, first, the false and, second, true revivals of religion. In the first of the two, Parker compared the apothecary shop filled with medicines to the stock of religions. One must have medicine or die; one must have religion or die; but the specific remedy is the whole problem—for there was a difference between oatmeal and strychnine. Parker described the stock of the religions by specifying acts done in their names, including the sacrifice of Isaac, the crucifixion of Christ, the persecution of Quakers, and the fanaticism of the revivals of 1858. These and many other cruel and inhuman acts have been committed in the name of religion.

To these examples he opposed a variety of virtuous acts and the beliefs of his own congregation. Their idea of religion put into practice would lead to a society without slavery, drunkenness, ignorance, prostitution, and war; for "creative love shall take the place of aggressive lust and repressive fear." For this transformation to occur, "The family, the community, the nation, the world, must be organized on justice, not on covetousness, fraud, and violence. . . ." A true revival of religion could lead to such a society, but such a revival would spring from the development of the religious faculty in individuals, since it could only come from a revival of piety and morality. The task of the minister was to promote the growth of the religious faculty in the individual: "But man is social. The individual alone is a wild man; it is only in society that noble individualism is instantially [sic] possible."[3] The individual could only accomplish his greatest achievement when society was not burdened by war, slavery, poverty, crime, the inferior condition of women, and the present corrupt state of the government. So the minister also had the task of diffusing ideas through the social order. Parker, who recognized how few accomplish this task, considered Emerson the man who has done most to promote the true revival of religion. Parker aspired to a like achievement of creating a true revival.

II *Historic Americans*

Seeking, himself, to lead men to a better society, and seldom succeeding conspicuously, Parker often examined the lives of acknowledged leaders. Among the last series of lectures which he gave is one published as *Historic Americans*, a set of four lectures on Franklin, Washington, John Adams, and Jefferson. Though given in 1858 when Parker was on the verge of a physical breakdown, caused in part from his work against slavery, these are not hastily composed essays intended merely to entertain or casually to praise. Each study was committed to paper only after extensive research and careful thought. Though a good number of Parker's sermons show careless haste of composition, his biographical lectures particularly reflect the hours he spent in research; and these were no exception though written during one of the busiest periods of his life.

In an introduction to an edition of these sketches, O. B. Frothingham noted that Parker wrote them in order to present principles important to the nation, to present the example of great men to his contemporaries, to present their lives truthfully without the myths that had grown up about them, to break the idol to reveal the man. As often, Frothingham came close to truth; but Parker was after something else which is less apparent: he was working with a vague foreknowledge that at best he would soon enter a period of inactivity, and one of the problems which teased him for years was that of finding the great Americans, of finding a pulse of the nation.

Parker did not believe as strongly as Emerson in the importance of biography, but he did believe in the greatness of the nation and in the necessity of great men arising in great nations. He wanted to find these men and to describe their greatness. Often he had been disappointed in American statesmen; often they had failed him as he looked to them for leadership. Of immediate importance was finding a candidate for the elections of 1860; and to find him Parker had to know what to look for—and he wanted others to be able to recognize greatness. These purposes led him to look to the supposedly great men of the past for characteristics which made a great statesman, and the results were his lectures on these four whom he admired most in the national history.

Since Parker's primary aim was not to judge each of the four, he did not rank them in their importance or conclude that one is greater than another. Each was considered individually and presented in two ways: each essay included a biographical section in which the most important facts and accomplishments were clearly outlined and another section in which the man's characteristics are evaluated. Franklin received Parker's highest praise: "Beyond all question, as I think, Benjamin Franklin had the largest mind that has shone this side of the sea,—widest in its comprehension, most deep-looking, thoughtful, far-seeing, of course the most original and creative child of the New World." Parker judged him on the basis of his intellect, his moral quality, his affectionate quality, and his religion. The intellect was composed of three capacities—understanding, imagination, reason; and Franklin was only less than great in imagination.

Though Parker recognized Franklin's personal moral shortcomings, he considered these secondary to the larger matters involving nations and humanity. His affectionate nature was revealed in his dealing with the world at large; "Franklin was the universal Good Samaritan." Parker could not resist devoting some space to Franklin's religion, since he knew his audience was critical of Franklin's Deism. But Parker did not share this opinion, for Franklin "had natural religion" however much he lacked a belief in creeds and doctrines. The only severe fault Parker found with Franklin was his failure during the Constitutional Convention to insist on the prohibition of slavery. But for the rest Parker could find no greater: he noted Franklin's contributions to science, to education, to statesmanship. His eminence lay in the breadth of his accomplishments.[4] Parker seldom failed to praise in others what he found or hoped to find in himself.

Washington presented problems Parker did not have to consider with Franklin, for he was a Virginian who owned slaves. But, rather than laboring over Washington's background, Parker emphasized the war, the New England support of it, and the Southern lack of support. Near the end of the lecture, Parker even described Washington as the least Southern of the great Virginians: "In character he is as much a New Englander as either Adams." In character, Washington lacked reason and imagination but not understanding; that is, he lacked ideas and an esthetic sense but not judgment. In Parker's scheme, Washington was an organizer rather than an originator—and this allowed him to lead the army and then the government. Parker could praise his religion and his morality but not, of course, his slaveholding. What Parker found most remarkable about Washington were his integrity and his sense of justice. He lacked Franklin's intellect and ideas but he was a great and humble leader.[5] Parker, who largely overlooked the aristocratic aspect of Washington and minimized his Virginian heritage, presented him as farmer rather than patrician, as President and general rather than aristocrat and slaveholder.

Parker, who had more trouble with John Adams than with the others, attempted to solve the problem by devoting more space to the biographical facts of Adams's life; but the effect was to present him as a working politician in the best sense. Looking

at Adams's character in the same terms in which he examined
the others, Parker found Adams to have had a great intellect
marked by good understanding, fair imagination, and great reason.
He was not a great organizer, a great inventor, nor a good administrator; but he was moral. It was the integrity of Adams to
which Parker returns again and again, while the list of faults
was longer for him than for any of the others. Even in religion
he was not the equal of Washington, Franklin, or Jefferson. In
each of these three, Parker found different qualities to praise
most highly; but none possessed all the qualities which Parker
valued. The biographical facts and significant achievements are
presented dispassionately, but the judgments of qualities are clear
reflections of Parker's own values.

The lecture on Jefferson opens not with the man but with his
state: New England was settled by Calvinists with progressive
ideas; Virginia was settled by aristocrats who did not want
democracy. All its institutions were, therefore, aristocratic, while
in New England education, politics, religion were in the hands
of the people. Of the three classes of men in Virginia—large
landholders, small proprietors, and poor whites—only the second
class produced distinguished men. Jefferson came from this class
and eventually led "the Progressive Party which was composed
of a few men of genius, of ideas, and strength, but chiefly made
up of the lower masses of men, with whom the instinct are
stronger than reflection, and the rich slaveholders of the South,
who liked not the constraints of law." Parker's criticism of the
party was that it did not have a high moral tone. He recounted
Jefferson's policies and accomplishments at great length, approving
of almost all of them. The man himself he found had great intellect because of his understanding rather than because of his
reason or imagination. He had moral courage, "But I think the
charge that he was father of some of his own slaves is but too
well founded." Yet Parker praised Jefferson's antislavery and
thought most highly of his belief in the people and in democracy.
He led the party which established democracy and began the
reforms still being carried out.[6] Had he known more of Jefferson's
extensive accomplishments and been able to forgive him for his
heritage, Parker might have found him second only to Franklin.
However, unable to like the man and unable to approve of his
relations with his slaves, Parker could only grudgingly admit his
accomplishments.

Despite the care with which Parker studied the lives of these men and presented their accomplishment and characters, he could not conclude that he had found either the typical American statesman or the great American politician. The man he thought greatest had never led the government, and the others had personal faults he could not overlook. Better than the men now in power, they yet were the best examples he could find rather than the best that could be. He was still looking for the future Christ he had predicted years before; he continued to find human beings. Though there is no specific admission of his disappointment at including two Virginians among the group, his efforts at avoiding the influence of the South on Washington and Jefferson are considerable. Believing as strongly as he does in the superiority of New England, Parker could not admit that some qualities had allowed Virginia to produce so many leaders in the early history of the nation; indeed, he does not even attempt an explanation of this contribution. Always presenting New Englanders as the leading people of the nation, he yet has to turn to the South to find the individual leaders; for he could not avoid history.

The scheme of evaluation which included intellect, moral quality, affectionate quality, and religion reveal much more of Parker than of the men of whom he wrote; for these qualities are the virtues for which Parker sought in himself as well as in others. None taken by itself can be identified as a trait of leadership. To be intelligent, moral, affectionate, and religious was to be good, perhaps even to be great in a particular sense; but it was not to be a statesman and a leader of men and nations. So righteous, moral, and humane was Theodore Parker that he identified the qualities to which he aspired and for which he looked in others with greatness. Without realizing it, Parker was forever doomed to separate the abstract and the practical. While he could write of the accomplishments of a Jefferson and recognize their greatness, he could not say that the man to whom they belonged was great. He searched for the statesman-saint, the future Christ, and did not find him.

III   *Autobiography*

With some justification one might say that in his search for greatness, Parker turned finally to himself. In April, 1859, he finished writing to his congregation a long letter entitled "Theodore Parker's Experience as a Minister." Sent from the West Indies, the letter was written after Parker had completed his career, though this fact was not certain at that time. He had left Boston in haste; "Consumption, having long since slain almost all my near kinsfolk, horsed on the north-wind, rode at me also, seeking my life."[7] Having some time and a little strength to complete his farewell, he decided to make it a full statement of his life and work, acknowledging as his audience all of mankind who wish to read it.

Recalling his youth, he especially remembered the problem of choosing a vocation. His choice between the ministry and the law was made on the ground that "the lawyer's moral tone was lower than the minister's." But he also confessed: "I dared not put myself under that temptation I prayed God not to lead me into." His reservations about the ministry sprang from his disappointment in the caliber of the clergymen he knew and from the little effect they seemed to have on their congregations. At the time he entered the Divinity School, he recalled that he decided to become a minister in order to help "the development of man's highest powers."[8] At this time he doubted the doctrines of eternal damnation, the trinity, the divinity of Christ, miracles, and plenary inspiration. These doubts are not so clear in his letters and journals of the 1830's, but his admission of them sheds light on the way in which Parker regarded his own course. He began with a strong sense of duty but with doubts of the theology under which he worked.

He remembered that, during the years of his education at Harvard, he came to believe in the immanence of God in man and to disbelieve in the authority of the Bible and the church. He rejected Locke and accepted the method of Kant, that of instinctive intuition. Freed from the old methods, he discovered how to find truth through induction from the facts of history and through deduction "from the primitive facts of consciousness." Obsessed with this freedom, he resolved to preach what he had come to know himself. He felt at home in the Unitarian Church, since its only distinctive doctrine was the denial of the Trinity. On leaving school, he was warned against settling in a small church since this would force him to publish his views through his writings in order to be heard. He paid great attention to the new ideas abroad in Boston; to the Unitarian controversies, and to the writings of the Germans, Carlyle, Wordsworth, Coleridge, and Cousin then being read in Boston. He was part of the "movement party" which started *The Dial* "wherein their wisdom and their folly rode together on the same saddle,"[9] one of the most refreshing descriptions of the journal. Without malice, he men-

tioned his battles with the Unitarian establishment and his difficulties in getting some of his work published.

Though the compression of his life's work in a few pages seems
to distort the order and dating of some of his ideas, particularly
those early in his life, Parker did give the accurate impression
that he very early arrived at some of the central doctrines of his
preaching. He arranged under three headings some of the ideas
which seem most important to him, and these were the "INFINITE
PERFECTION OF GOD," "THE ADEQUACY OF MAN FOR ALL HIS
FUNCTIONS," and "ABSOLUTE OR NATURAL RELIGION" [10] Parker
apologized for the abstract qualities of these doctrines and asserted
that "they must take a concrete form, and be applied to the actual
life of the individual family, community, state, and church." This
work, after all, was his great contribution: the attempt to trans-
mute these doctrines into reality. As he clearly revealed in his last
sermons, the attempt became firmly rooted in the belief of man's
reliance upon community—that men could not achieve virtue outside of community. In his autobiographical work he said that to apply and spread his doctrines he looked for the sources of power and
found them to be the "trading power," the "political power," the
"ecclesiastical power," and the "literary power." But, since none
of these were accessible to him, it seemed to him that all the
power structures were closed to him.

It was first in his attempts to do something for "the perishing
and dangerous classes" that he realized the effect of those who
worked against him. He could do little openly but had to work
through others to accomplish his aims: "I sometimes saw my
scheme prosper, and read my words in the public reports, while
the whole enterprise had been ruined at once if my face or name
had appeared in connection with it." Some of the activities which
occupied most of his time, such as his work in helping fugitive
slaves escape to Canada, are forever lost because of his secrecy.
Even in this extensive autobiographical account he did not reveal
all of the things in which he participated.

Parker said he never wished to lecture broadly, but the forces
amassed against him caused him to lecture and to publish wherever
he could in order to be heard. That he could publish and lecture,
that he could be heard, suggests not that the enemies were weak
but that they were not so numerous or so malicious as Parker
supposed. At any rate, the issue of slavery also led him to lecture
extensively. The institution of the lecture gave him a freedom he

did not have in the pulpit or in many publications, for he could virtually say what he wished. Here he could pursue his efforts to lead the nation away from slavery to freedom "which leads at once to industrial democracy—respect for labor, government over all, by all, for the sake of all, rule after the eternal right as it is writ in the constitution of the universe—securing welfare and progress." He recalled lecturing from eighty to a hundred times a year for ten years to about sixty thousand people a year. His own estimate of is influence was that "scarcely any American, not holding a political office, has touched the minds of so many men, by freely speaking on matters of the greatest impor- tance. . . ."[11] Often he spoke as the martyr who could not be heard while proudly describing the huge audiences which did in fact hear him.

Parker listed eight "prominent evils" against which he has preached—intemperance, covetousness, ignorance, the condition of women, improper politics, war, slavery, and false theology. Since these efforts were to educate men for true religion and to promote the general welfare, he always "endeavoured to establish philosophically the moral principle . . . and show its origin in the constitution of man, to lay down the natural law . . . ; to show what welfare had followed in human history from keeping this law, and what misery from violating it; . . ." and apply the prin- ciple to the evil. Parker explained more clearly in this letter than elsewhere his view of the problem of the desire for property. Sometimes he had seemed to point to capitalism as the evil responsible for poverty, but he here specified that it was the excessive and uncontrolled desire for property that is evil. The desire for property was itself not bad: "In this generation, the productive industry of New-England seems vulgar to careless eyes, and excessive to severe ones; but it is yet laying the material and indispensable foundation for a spiritual civilization in some future age, more grand, I think, than mankind has hitherto rejoiced in."[12] He looked forward to an affluent society in which property would be widely distributed.

No mere summary of this "Letter" can do justice to its range and complexity, and one wishing to know Parker better must read through its hundred pages. In his customary simple style he set out his life and ambitions in brief and in fair and reasonable proportions. The earnest and defensive tone is characteristic of all his writings and actions—as are his descriptions of his enemies and his frequent failure to mention his friends; for Parker wished to become a persecuted saint, a new Christ such as he spoke of early in his career, and the "Letter" is a last effort to accomplish that. In the "Letter" he sketched the course of his life, but the real failure and frustrations which are missing are so clear and so inevitable that most of them did not need to be specified. They were his failure to have a child, to end slavery and the other evils against which he preached, and to establish in some tangible form the results of the theology over which he labored. The sizable pride which he always possessed and could not hide is painfully revealed as Parker specifies his ambition and ignores his failures. By 1859 the evils which he acknowledged as his primary targets stood almost as firmly as when he began. But Abolition was more acceptable in Boston in 1859 than it had been in 1840, and the while nation was responding to slavery as a real issue. Parker—through his work against slavery; against weak, subservient politicians; and against the old theology—had effected changes in men's minds if not in the social fabric.

IV *John Brown*

Though Parker had left the United States early in 1859, one particular work which he had helped to launch did not come to fruition until later that year when John Brown made his famous— or infamous—raid at Harper's Ferry. Parker, who had been supporting Brown for some time, was one of the Secret Six giving him the aid to make this raid. The precise nature of Parker's aid to Brown and the extent of his knowledge of Brown's plans may never be fully known. Parker—in Rome when he heard that Brown was to be hanged on December 2—wrote that he wished he could be home to speak in defense of Brown; perhaps he envisaged another *Defence*. But he could at least express his ideas to his friends at home. Without admitting his own support of Brown, he wrote the letter entitled "John Brown's Expedition Reviewed."

From Parker's belief in freedom and the necessity for community, he argued that the slave had a right to kill those who keep him enslaved and that the free man had a right to help the slave gain his freedom. This second point he considered to be so clear that it needed no argument. Cautiously, he wondered if it might be the duty of the free man to help the slave by killing those who enslaved him. This duty was controlled by the possible and by the relations within a community; in other words, there was some question about the duty of helping slaves in Africa but none concerning the slaves in Virginia. Quite probably the end of slavery in America would only come with bloodshed, since "All the great charters of HUMANITY have been writ in blood." Parker saw Brown as using one method to achieve the desired end; the Anti-Slavery Society, another. The slaves themselves might soon rise if white men appeared to lead them.

Parker still believed in the inferiority of the Negro who did not have the "instinct for liberty" common among Caucasians. He also feared the "Africanization of America" which would be possible as long as slavery continued. Democracy and the rights of free men could only be preserved and extended by ending slavery. This end would come through peaceful means or through violence, but it would come. Parker had nothing but praise for Captain John Brown who chose violence,[13] and Parker himself was ready to accept as duty the violent abolition of slavery. Had he lived to see the Civil War, there is no doubt of his acceptance of that, despite his youthful condemnation of war.

Parker, like most of the Transcendentalists, had a set of objections to slavery which were scarcely based on humanitarian grounds. They did not particularly wish to see Negroes throughout the land enjoying the rights of other free men, and they did not wish to see the Negro free on humanitarian grounds. They did not oppose Negro slavery. The Negro was the subject and accessory to the sin of slavery. They wished the abolition of slavery for the extension of democracy, the rights of man, and the salvation of the nation. They had virtually no faith in what Negroes as a race or as individuals could contribute to the nation; they considered them inferior, though Parker was one of the few to state this view in such unequivocal terms.

V   *Recent Estimates*

Two of the most careful brief considerations of Parker are given by R. W. B. Lewis and V. L. Parrington, each of whom presents Parker within the context of a rather elaborate scheme. Lewis, who describes Parker as "an American Rabelais" and "an American Luther," charges him with wishing "to remove religion from the context of history altogether." Looking at a sermon such as "The Transient and the Permanent in Christianity," one can readily conclude that Parker wished to strip religion of its history and to focus on what he considered its enduring, its permanent, its non-institutional aspects. (As Lewis notes, this procedure is typically American.) However, Parker emphasized history in both his religious and his social sermons: in sermons and lectures given during his whole lifetime, he mentioned the history of institutions; time after time he gave the history of slavery in the United States. Theodore Parker did not deny history; on the contrary, he continually and fully recognized it; but, rather than building upon it, he wished to escape it. Christianity should purge itself of its history; the nation should rid itself of the burdens imposed by history; for Parker regarded each man as a new individual. As Lewis puts it, "Theodore Parker was the one to come up with the breath-taking suggestion that every individual was in spirit and in fact a perfectly new man, as new as Adam, each the first man, each the new unfallen." [14]

Parker himself might not have been willing to accept such a description of his views. Parker would emphasize the potential of man rather than his current state; his ability, rather than his accomplishment; his future, rather than his past. Yet he would prefer the image of the Adam before the fall since he could not accept the doctrine of the fall and its consequences, just as he could not accept the orthodox concepts of sin and atonement. To Parker, the search for perfection springs from perfection.

Yet beyond this concept is a correlative not embodied in an Adamic notion: for Parker, there was no greatness in the individual alone; and man could not reach perfection alone. As Parker clearly indicated in his "Experience," the community, from the family to the nation, was the key to the elevation of the society. So often has Transcendentalism been mistakenly identified with the Adam Smith type of individualism that the strong emphasis placed on community by Parker and a few others has been neglected. When Parker wrote of ending slavery, reforming drunkards, reducing poverty, and practicing absolute religion, he implied that from these corrections would come not only better individuals but also a better society. Parker preached to individuals to improve their society, and the goal of an industrial democracy for which Parker worked for many years reveals this emphasis in his vision: he sought a national community composed of virtuous individuals, democratic in politics, and industrialized in its economic organization.

To Parrington, Parker "became the embodiment and epitome of the New England renaissance." The three characteristics of the time that Parker represented were "the idealistic theism implicit in the Unitarian reaction from Calvinism; the transcendental individualism latent in the doctrine of divine immanence; and the passion for righteousness, to make the will of God prevail in a world where the devil quite openly kept his ledgers."[15] Parrington's flair for generalization and the carefully well-turned phrase do not serve him well here. It is true that Parker developed certain ideas of Unitarianism to a logical conclusion, that the doctrine of divine immanence was quite central for him, and that he did have a passion for righteousness. But he went further than the Unitarians wished or intended to go, and he would not accord to the devil so much as his commentator does. Parker's contribution is not that he represented Transcendentalism or the New England renaissance; for everything he turned to he intentionally and consciously carried a few steps beyond.

Though it is penurious to charge, as Lewis does, that Parker finally had little to say, the assertion must be frankly considered. Parker, despite his own strong desires, was a doer rather than an original thinker. He was a voice, a man of action. When he took the South Boston sermon, which became his most famous theological statement, to George Ripley, they agreed it was neither very original nor very well written. Yet much of Parker's career followed from it. When he chose to do a translation for what would be seen as his greatest achievement in scholarship, he completed a work of erudition which must be regarded as a secondary work despite his extensive additions. When he turned to sociological analysis, he followed Orestes Brownson to a large degree. When he preached and lectured against slavery, he gave new forms to what others had already said; and he came late to the work.

Emerson called Parker "our Savonarola." The association aptly characterizes Parker as a moral reformer, as a "patriot-priest." Like Savonarola, Parker sought to reform church and nation. Conscious of the ideals held in the culture, he spent his life trying to achieve that perfection. His achievement was in describing these ideals and the reality from which they grew. He advanced the changes in Unitarianism, and he helped lead the antislavery forces in Boston; these accomplishments have been generally recognized. He should also be seen as a man who in his writings and in his actions represents the early and the late nineteenth-century American moral reformer who is confident of attainable national perfection. He belongs on the list of Americans—liberal and conservative—from the seventeenth century to the twentieth century who insist that the millennium will come soon.

Parker's belief in the destiny of America—"manifest destiny" to the nineteenth century—was chauvinistic, but it was grounded in a religious belief. For him, America was destined to become the leading nation on earth. The economic-political system, industrial democracy, that he saw as the only viable system has been generally accepted as the firm basis for present and future national success. Parker, then, embodied the beliefs which have become deeply ingrained in national thought. As the decades have passed, Parker has come to seem less the radical extremist; he has come to represent a normative American.

Notes and References

Chapter One

1. "An Autobiographical Fragment," *The Collected Works of Theodore Parker,* Centenary Edition (Boston, 1907-10), XIII, 10. Hereafter cited as *Works* (Centenary).
2. Quoted in John Weiss, *Life and Correspondence of Theodore Parker* (London, 1863), I, 24, 21.
3. Weiss, I, 50. Dr. Samuel Gridley Howe (1801-1876), the husband of Julia Ward Howe, was a physician, reformer and teacher. A close friend and Abolitionist associate of Parker, he is now best known as a teacher of the blind.
4. Ibid., I, 57. Constance Rourke includes a chapter on Beecher in her *Trumpets of Jubilee* (New York, 1927).
5. Octavius Brooks Frothingham, *Theodore Parker* (Boston, 1874), p. 37.
6. Frothingham, p. 38.
7. Frothingham, pp. 44-46.
8. Weiss, I, 67.
9. John White Chadwick, *Theodore Parker* (Boston, 1900), p. 39.
10. Weiss, I, 77.
11. *Scriptural Interpreter,* V (1835), 229, 251.
12. Ibid., VII (1837), 270. Parker once wrote a self guide in which he reminded himself to:
    Preserve devoutness by,—
    1. Contemplation of Nature;
    2. Of the attributes of God;
    3. Of my own dependence.
    4. By prayer at night and morn, and at all times when devout feelings come over me. (Frothingham, p. 49.)
13. Weiss, I, 96. During the month he spent at Barnstable, Parker thought he had become a man, not just a student: "A

mere student is a sort of *homunculus,* an animal not treated
by Pliny, except incidentally, when he speaketh of the war
they once carried on against their arch enemies the cranes."
Frothingham, p. 73.

14. The problem of resolving the value of study (a function of
the Understanding) with the value of intuition (a function of
the Reason) has been noticed by historians of the movement.
As one scholar puts it, "This picture of this ardent transcendentalist systematically ransacking the facts of history
with the tools of science in order to prove his intuitive truths
is no without its comic character." Another comments more
reverently, "The function of the understanding in relation to
reason . . . is obvious; it is to present concepts to the reason
for final verdict." Both views are tenable, but it is difficult to
be certain of the resolution of the Transcendentalists. Parker
and others spoke and wrote to convince others of the truths
they reached intuitively. The apparent paradox of the functions of Reason and Understanding did not disturb them. On
the relations of Reason and Understanding for Parker, see
John Edward Dirks, *The Critical Theology of Theodore
Parker* (New York, 1948), pp. 133ff and George F. Newbrough, "Reason and Understanding of the Works of Theodore Parker," *South Atlantic Quarterly,* XLVII (January,
1948), 64-75.

15. Weiss, I, 96, 98.

16. Frothingham, pp. 78-79.

17. Quoted in John Weiss, *Discourse Occasioned by the Death of
Convers Francis* (Cambridge, 1963), p. 28.

Chapter Two

1. The third volume of the *Literary History of the United States*
(New York, 1959), pp. 346-48, contains a bibliography of
Transcendentalism. Other recent works to be consulted
include studies and biographies of Emerson and Thoreau,
Perry Miller, *The Transcendentalists* (Cambridge, 1950) and
William R. Hutchison, *The Transcendentalist Ministers* (New
Haven, 1959).

2. *Christian Examiner,* XXVI (May, 1839), 269.

3. *Ibid.,* XXVII (July, 1840), 273-316.

4. Frothingham, p. 106.
5. Weiss, I, 119.
6. Andrews Norton, *A Discourse on the Latest Form of Infidelity* (Cambridge, 1839), pp. 22, 53, 58. Though Norton has often been portrayed as a bigoted opponent of Transcendentalism, he was an important scholar.
7. [George Ripley], *"The Latest Form of Infidelity" Examined* (Boston, 1839), pp. 12-13, 115-16.
8. Weiss, I, 153.
9. The clipping may be found in Parker's journal (1838), p. 32; it is from *The Boston Daily Advertiser,* Monday, August 27, 1838. Norton's letter is reprinted in Miller, pp. 193-96.
10. Miller, p. 230.
11. For an excellent discussion of this matter, see Clarence H. Faust, "The Background of the Unitarian Opposition to Transcendentalism," *Modern Philology,* XXXV (February, 1938), 297-324.
12. For information on this institution, see Charles Lyttle, "An Outline of the History of the Berry Street Ministerial Conference," *Meadville Theological School Quarterly Bulletin,* XXIV (July, 1930), 3-27.
13. Parker, Journal (1840), p. 387; Weiss, I, 155.
14. Weiss, I, 157. (The italicized words refer to books Parker expected to write.)
15. *The Dial,* I (July, 1840), 58-70.
16. Weiss, I, 158.
17. Weiss, I, 144.
18. Frothingham, p. 95.
19. *West Roxbury Sermons* (Boston, 1892), p. 23.
20. Weiss, I, 167.
21. Chadwick, p. 98.
22. Miller, pp. 284-86, 291.
23. *Ibid.,* pp. 262ff.
24. Chadwick, p. 102; Henry Steele Commager, *Theodore Parker* (Boston, 1960), p. 76.
25. Weiss, I, 187.
26. Frothingham, p. 157.
27. Weiss, I, 170ff.
28. *Ibid.,* Weiss, I, 175-77.

Chapter Three

1. For an account of *The Dial* and its contributors see George Willis Cooke, *An Historical and Biographical Introduction to Accompany The Dial* (Cleveland, 1902), 2vv. and Clarence Gohdes, *The Periodicals of American Transcendentalism* (Durham, 1931), esp. pp. 8ff.

2. Thomas W. Higginson, *Margaret Fuller Ossoli* (Boston, 1884), pp. 130, 165, 169. Parker privately responded to Emerson's praise of an article in *The Dial*. "He said it was full of life. But, alas! the life is Emerson's and not _____'s, and so it had been lived before." Weiss, I, 125.

3. *The Dial,* II (July, 1841), 59-76. Schlesinger notes that Brownson believed Parker was plagiarizing his work in "A Lesson for the Day.? Arthur M. Schlesinger, Jr., *Orestes A. Brownson* (Boston, 1939), p. 104.

4. "Christianity," *The Dial,* II (January, 1842), 292-313; "Thoughts on Theology," *The Dial,* II (April, 1842), 485-528.

5. *The Dial,* I (January, 1841), 315-39.

6. While Parker freely used humor in his journal, he seldom did so in his published work. It emerges in this article for *The Dial* and in a few other places including his last article, "A Bumblebee's Thoughts" (*Works* [Centenary], IV, 425). Cooke describes Parker's final article in his note at the end of the volume (p. 482): "It was meant as an attack on the methods of Paley and the Bridgewater treatises. It also has an element of humor that is most interesting as well as keenly satirical."

7. *The Dial,* I (April, 1841), 497-519.

8. Schlesingter (p. 104) describes the article as "full of diluted Brownsonism, the vigor lost in a mass of bad rhetoric and irrelevant erudition." Though Parker may have started with Brownson's ideas, he did not merely repeat them. But it is true that the style of this article is often unsatisfactory and that Brownson was in 1841 at least a more perceptive social critic than Parker. The fable of the village of Humdrum is one of the best sections of the article.

9. Weiss, I, 184. The contradictions between Parker's resolution to work through the press (1837) and his later complaint about preaching in West Roxburg (1842) need not be re-

solved. The new decision surely was based in part on the realization that his ambition required him to have a potentially larger audience.

For further information on Brook Farm, see Henry W. Sams (ed.), *Autobiography of Brook Farm* (Englewood Cliffs, N. J., 1958), an excellent sourcebook.

10. *Works* (Centenary), I, II 33, 81, 94, 102. Also, *The Collected Works of Theodore Parker,* ed. Frances P. Cobbe (London, 1863-74), I, 8, 7, 24, 59. Hereafter cited as *Works* (Cobbe). Parker wanted "to imbed religion in the very structure of the human soul." R. W. B. Lewis, *The American Adam* (Chicago, 1955), p. 179.

11. *Works* (Centenary), I, 152, 159, 183; *Works (*Cobbe), I, 111, 116, 133.

12. *Ibid.,* I, 295; *Works* (Cobbe), I, 216.

13. *Ibid.,* I, 406; *Works* (Cobbe), I, 299.

14. "An Humble Tribute to the Memory of William Ellery Channing, D.D.," in Theodore Parker, *Views of Religion,* 5th ed. (Boston, 1900), p. 383.

15. *Works* (Centenary), I, 415-19, 427; *Works* (Cobbe), I, 306-09, 315.

16. *Boston Quarterly Review,* V (October, 1842), 437. Brownson tried to summarize Parker's work: "Here is the essence of Mr. Parker's whole doctrine. Man is created perfect. He is created with religious wants. There is a supply for those wants. If he is perfect he must have the natural ability to obtain that supply. Hence no need of supernatural aid to direct him to the supply, nor to enable him when discovered to possess himself of it. Here we have this novel theory, which this volume of five hundred and three pages was written to bring out and establish. The great aim of the author is everywhere apparent,—it is to get rid of supernaturalism."

17. Journal, pp. 241ff; Weiss, I, 188ff. The right of free inquiry was one on which the Unitarians prided themselves. In appealing to this right, Parker was challenging one of the accepted principles on which the Unitarians agreed.

18. *A Critical and Historical Introduction to the Canonical Scriptures of the Old Testament* (Boston, 1843).

19. Dirks, pp. 35, 57, 43.

20. Weiss, I, 201.

21. *Ibid.,* I, 203.
22. *Ibid.,* I, 232.
23. *Ibid.,* I, 235.
24. Frothingham, p. 214.
25. *Ibid.,* pp. 218-30.
26. Octavius Brooks Frothingham, *Boston Unitarianism* (Boston, 1890), pp. 45, 55-57.
27. *Ibid.,* pp. 57, 101, 193.

Chapter Four

1. "Some Account of My Ministry," *Works* (Centenary), XIII, 50-82; *Works* (Cobbe), XII, 190-214.
 2. Frothingham, pp. 231-36. "The True Idea of a Christian Church," *Works* (Centenary), XIII, 17-49; *Works* (Cobbe), III, 36-60.
 3. Frothingham, pp. 241-50; Chadwick, pp. 200-204.
 4. For a description of Parker's preaching, see Frothingham, pp. 340-42; for further description of the Music Hall services, see Chadwick, pp. 209ff.
 5. Frothingham, p. 383.
 6. "War," *Works* (Centenary), IX, 288-325; *Works* (Cobbe), IV, 1-31.
 7. "The Mexican War," *Works* (Centenary), XII, 1-47; "A Sermon of the Mexican War," *Works* (Cobbe), IV, 41-76.
 8. "The Mexican War," *Works* (Centenary), XI, 21-31; "Speech Delivered at the Anti-War Meeting," *Works* (Cobbe), IV, 32-40.
 9. "The Perishing Classes," *Works* (Centenary), X, 103-36; "A Sermon of the Perishing Classes in Boston," *Works* (Cobbe), VII, 34-59.
10. "Poverty," *Works* (Centenary), IX, 263-87; "A Sermon of Poverty," *Works* (Cobbe), VII, 94-113.
11. "The Dangerous Classes," *Works* (Centenary), X, 137-79; "A Sermon of the Dangerous Classes in Society," *Works* (Cobbe), VII, 60-93.
12. "The Mercantile Classes," *Works* (Centenary), X, 1-41; "A Sermon of Merchants," *Works* (Cobbe), VII, 1-33.
13. "Spiritual Conditions," *Works* (Centenary), X, 292-334; "A Sermon of the Spiritual Condition of Boston," *Works* (Cobbe), VII, 146-79.

14. "The Chief Sins of the People," *Works* (Centenary), IX, 1-48; *Works* (Cobbe), VII, 257-95.
15. "The American Scholar," *Works* (Centenary), VIII, 1-53; "The Positions and Duties of the American Scholar," *Works* (Cobbe), VII, 217-56. Cf. George William Curtis, "The Duty of the American Scholar to Politics and the Times," *Orations and Addresses* (New York, 1893), I, 3-35 and Ralph Waldo Emerson, "The American Scholar," *Works* (Boston, 1883), I, 83-115.
16. "The Public Education of the People," *Works* (Centenary), IX, 91-139; *Works* (Cobbe), VII, 180-216.
17. Ralph Rusk, *The Life of Ralph Waldo Emerson* (New York, 1949), p. 324. Theodore Parker to Horace Mann, May 15, 1847, Mann Collection, Massachusetts Historical Society. Theodore Parker to Ralph Waldo Emerson, June 20, 1847 and August 30, 1847, Emerson Collection, Houghton Library, Harvard University. The reason for some of the difficulties of the *Massachusetts Quarterly Review* was given by one of Parker's contemporaries, T. W. Higginson, as follows: "He [Parker] was a hard man to relieve, to help or to cooperate with. Thus, the 'Massachusetts Quarterly Review' his especial organ, began with a promising corps of contributors; but when it appeared that its editor, if left alone, would willingly undertake all the articles,—science, history, literature, everything,— of course the others yielded to inertia and dropped away." Thomas Wentworth Higginson, *Contemporaries* (Boston, 1899), p. 41.
18. Gohdes, pp. 191-93.
19. *Massachusetts Quarterly Review,* I (December, 1847), 8-54.
20. *Ibid.,* I (June, 1848), 331-76.
21. "William Ellery Channing," *Massachusetts Quarterly Review,* I (September, 1848), 423-55.
22. *Massachusetts Quarterly Review,* II (December, 1848), 1-31.
23. *Ibid.,* 105-26. The abolitionist, William Lloyd Garrison is "the one agitator."
24. "Mr. Prescott as Historian," *Massachusetts Quarterly Review,* II (March, 1849), 215-48.
25. *Massachusetts Quarterly Review,* II (September, 1849), 437-70.
26. *Ibid.,* III (December, 1849), 118-57. Parker wrote a sixteen-

page manuscript titled "The People, an Opera, in one Act." The speakers include slave-owners, office holders, office seekers of both the Whig and Locofoco parties, the Cabinet, Polk—as the villain—and the People, the heroic force that demands an end to the Mexican War and the taxes which support it. After Polk promises "new Territory in South, North and West" including all of North and South America, the people rebuke him, "Hold hold, enough, / All that is Stuff." The manuscript has never been printed; it was generously given to the author by Prof. Charles H. Foster.

27. "The Writings of R. W. Emerson," *Massachusetts Quarterly Review,* III (March, 1850), 200-55.
28. *Massachusetts Quarterly Review,* III (June, 1850), 386-425.
29. *Ibid.,* III (September, 1850), 512-23.

Chapter Five

1. *Works* (Centenary), XI, 1-20; *Works* (Cobbe), V, 1-16.
2. "The Abolition of Slavery by the French Republic," *Works* (Centenary), XI, 165-75; "Speech at a Meeting of the American Anti-Slavery Society," *Works* (Cobbe), V, 85-92.
3. "The Anti-Slavery Convention," *Works* (Centenary), XI, 176-88; "Speech at Faneuil Hall, Before the New England Anti-Slavery Convention," *Works* (Cobbe), V.
4. *A Letter to the People of the United States Touching The Matter of Slavery* (Boston, 1848), pp. 5-9. Reprinted in *Works* (Centenary), XI, 32-119 and in *Works* (Cobbe), V, 17-84.
5. *A Letter,* pp. 110-11.
6. *A Letter,* pp. 116, 119, 120.
7. Weiss, II, 79-84.
8. *Theodore Parker's Review of Webster* (Boston, 1850), pp. 19, 21, 23, 25. Reprinted in *Works* (Centenary), XI, 218-47 and in *Works* (Cobbe), VI, 212-34.
9. "The Slave Power," *Works* (Centenary), XI, 248-86; "Speech at the New England Anti-Slavery Convention," *Works* (Cobbe), V, 103-33.
10. "A Discourse Occasioned by the Death of the Late President Taylor," *Works* (Cobbe), IV, 184-211.
11. "The Function of Conscience," *Works* (Centenary), XI, 287-315; "The Function and Place of Conscience in Relation to

the Laws of Men: A Sermon for the Times," *Works* (Cobbe), V, 134-63.

12. "The State of the Nation," *Works* (Centenary), XII, 92-181; *Works* (Cobbe), IV, 235-65.

13. The Boston Committee of Vigilance was formed to combat the Fugitive Slave Law, according to some sources; but its date of origin is placed at various dates from 1842 to 1850. Theodore Parker was on the Executive Committee in 1850.

14. Frothingham, pp. 409-12.

15. "Speech at the Ministerial Conference in Boston," *Works* (Cobbe), V. To his Shaker friend, Robert White, Parker wrote that he thought too much weight had been put on Christ's words on non-resistance. Since Christ believed the world would soon end, he could easily council his listeners not to resist evil and to take no thought for the following day. Parker believed violence had its place; he would use force to aid a fugitive, for example. Weiss, I, 392-93.

16. Weiss, II, 112; Frothingham, p. 348.

17. "The Boston Kidnapping," *Works* (Centenary), XI, 316-85; *Works* (Cobbe), V, 172-224.

18. *Works* (Centenary), II, 196, 205. For his definitions of the varieties of atheism, see pp. 60, 87. The work is volume XI of the Cobbe edition.

19. "The Nebraska Question. Some Thoughts on the New Assault Upon Freedom in America," *Works* (Cobbe), V, 245-96.

20. Weiss, II, 226.

21. *Ibid.,* II, 206.

22. Frothingham, p. 445.

23. "The Progress of America," *Works* (Centenary), XII, 196-249; "Some Thoughts on the Progress of America, And the Influence of Her Diverse Institutions," *Works* (Cobbe), VI, 1-43.

24. Samuel Shapiro, "The Rendition of Anthony Burns," *Journal of Negro History,* XLIV (January, 1959), 34-51.

25. *The Liberator,* XXIVI (June 2, 1954).

26. "The New Crime Against Humanity," *Works* (Centenary), XII, 250-332; *Works* (Cobbe), VI, 44-109.

27. "The Law of God and the Statutes of Men," *Works* (Centenary), XIV 137-62; *Works* (Cobbe), V, 225-44.

28. *A Sermon of the Dangers Which Threaten the Rights of Man*

in America (Boston, 1854), pp. 19, 24. Reprinted, *Works* (Centenary), XII, 333-96.

29. *The Trial of Theodore Parker, for the "Misdemeanor" of a Speech in Faneuil Hall Against Kidnapping, before the Circuit Court of the United States* (Boston, 1855), pp. v, vii, 171-72, 1-2, 4, 9, 17, 156, 210, 218.

30. Weiss, I, 362.

31. *Ibid.,* II, 207-8.

32. In a letter of November 16, 1857, Parker stated that the Negro "in twenty generations . . . will stand just where [he] is now." He thought the race inferior, as proven by their inability to rise even into the middle class in Massachusetts though they possessed freedom. Frothingham, p. 467.

33. *The Great Battle Between Slavery and Freedom* (Boston, 1856), pp. 41, 76, 88.

34. "A New Lesson for the Day," *Works* (Centenary), XIV, 229-70; *Works* (Cobbe), IV, 279-311.

35. Weiss, II, 191.

36. *Ibid.,* I, 305.

37. *Ibid.,* I, 305.

38. "The Present Aspect of Slavery," *Works* (Centenary), XIV, 271-316; "The Present Aspect of Slavery in America, and the Immediate Duty of the North," *Works* (Cobbe), VI, 287-323, Weiss, II, 230.

39. Weiss, II, 240-41.

40. *Ibid.,* I, 396.

Chapter Six

1. "False and True Theology," *Works* (Centenary) IV, 342-64; *Works* (Cobbe), III, 257-73.

2. "A False and True Revival of Religion," *Works* (Centenary) IV, 365-90; *Works* (Cobbe), III, 211-30.

3. "The Revival We Need," *Works* (Centenary), IV, 391-424; "The Revival of Religion Which We Need," *Works* (Cobbe), III, 231-56.

4. "Benjamin Franklin," *Works* (Centenary), VII, 1-40; "Franklin," *Works* (Cobbe), XIII, 11-58.

5. "George Washington," *Works* (Centenary), VII, 41-96; "Washington," *Works* (Cobbe), XIII, 59-114.

6. "Thomas Jefferson," *Works* (Centenary), VII, 158-203; *Works* (Cobbe), XIII, 179-226.

7. *Theodore Parker's Experience as a Minister* (Boston, 1859), p. 26. Reprinted in *Works* (Centenary), XIII, 273-413; *Works* (Cobbe), XII, 252-356; and in *Theodore Parker: An Anthology,* ed. Henry Steele Commager (Boston, 1960), pp. 323-87.

8. *Experience,* pp. 33, 35.

9. *Experience,* pp. 43, 58.

10. *Experience,* pp. 78ff.

11. *Experience,* pp. 97, 99, 104.

12. *Experience, pp.* 117-118, 121.

13. "John Brown's Expedition Reviewed," *Works* (Cobbe), XII, 164-76.

14. R. W. B. Lewis, *The American Adam* (Chicago, 1955), p. 183.

15. Vernon L. Parrington, *Main Currents in American Thought* (New York, 1954), II, 408.

Selected Bibliography

PRIMARY SOURCES

1. *Bibliographies*

Chadwick, John White. *Theodore Parker: Preacher and Reformer*. Boston and New York: Houghton, Mifflin and Company, 1900, pp. xi-xx. Excellent bibliography of primary source material.

Commager, Henry Steele. *Theodore Parker*. Boston: Little, Brown and Company, 1936, pp. 311-31. A lengthy list of primary and secondary materials in essay form.

Literary History of the United States, ed. by Spiller, Thorp Johnson and Canby. New York: Macmillan Company, 1948, pp. III, 678-80. *Bibliography Supplement,* ed. Richard M. Ludwig (1959).

Wendte, Charles W. *Bibliography and Index to the Works of Theodore Parker*. Boston: Beacon Press, 1910, XV, 11-50. Includes a lengthy list of memorial articles.

2. *Texts*

Parker's complete writings are out of print and unavailable in many libraries. A very few essays and sermons have been reprinted in whole or in part in such works as Perry Miller's *The Transcendentalists* (1950) and Conrad Wright's *Three Prophets of Religious Liberalism* (1961). The list below consists of the collected editions and major works not included in either of those editions. No edition of the letters has been published, but the biographies by Frothingham and Weiss include many.

The Collected Works of Theodore Parker, ed. by Frances P. Cobbe. 14 vols. London: Trübner and Co., 1863-1874. Very uneven and incomplete. No. footnotes, no index, no bibliography. Yet occasionally more reliable than the following edition.

The Works of Theodore Parker. "Centenary Edition." 15 vols. Boston: American Unitarian Association, 1907-1913. Somewhat more satisfactory than the Cobbe edition because some volumes have useful introductions and notes, but it is not a complete collection and the eratic footnoting, changes of titles and numerous other inconsistencies mar the work.

Theodore Parker: An Anthology, ed. by Henry Steele Commager. Boston: Beacon Press, 1960. A very well-organized collection of excerpts from Parker's writings.

West Roxbury Sermons, 1334-1484. Boston: American Unitarian Association, 1902. Collection of early sermons not reprinted elsewhere.

Levi Blodgett Letter. The Previous Question. Boston: Weeks, Jordan, and Co., 1840. (Reprinted in Dirks, pp. 137-159.)

A Critical and Historical Introduction to the Canonical Scriptures of the Old Testament. 2 vols. Boston: Charles C. Little and James Brown, 1843. Parker's primary contribution to scholarship, based on a study in German by Wilhelm M. L. De Wette.

The Trial of Theodore Parker for the Misdemeanor . . . with the Defence. Boston: Pub. for the author, 1855.

3. *Manuscripts*

The important collections of Parker manuscripts are in the Boston Public Library (which also has Parker's library) and the Massachusetts Historical Society; each has over twenty volumes of material. Additional manuscripts are held by the Houghton Library of Harvard University and the American Unitarian Association. Holdings in the libraries include letters, notebooks, journals, sermons, lectures, clippings, scrapbooks and posters. The biographers have taken full advantage of this material. These Boston area libraries hold manuscript collections of other Transcendentalists and Unitarians that contain material relevant to the study of Parker.

SECONDARY SOURCES

AARON, DANIEL. *Men of Good Hope.* New York: Oxford University Press, 1951, esp. pp. 21-51. Emphasizes, as no other scholar does, Parker's concept of "industrial democracy" and other aspects of his economic and political philosophy.

ALCOTT, LOUISA M. *Work*. Boston: Roberts Brothers, 1873. Thomas Power, the minister in this novel, is Theodore Parker, whom Miss Alcott knew and admired.

ATKINS, GAIUS GLENN, and FREDERICK L. FAGLEY. *History of American Congregationalism*. Boston and Chicago: The Pilgrim Press, 1942. Chapter nine is a brief account of the Unitarian split from Congregationalism.

CHADWICK, JOHN WHITE. *Theodore Parker: Preacher and Reformer*. Boston and New York. Houghton, Mifflin and Company, 1950. A fine, sympathetic biography that emphasizes Parker's place in the theological battles.

COMMAGER, HENRY STEELE. "The Dilemma of Theodore Parker," *New England Quarterly*, VI (1933), 257-77. Interpretive description of Parker's dilemma between intuition and experience.

———. "Tempest in a Boston Teacup," *New England Quarterly*, VI (1933), 651-675. A discussion of the Blodgett letter and the controversey over miracles.

———. "Theodore Parker, Intellectual Gourmand," *American Scholar*, III (1934), 257-65. Describes Parker's library and his reading and asserts the primacy of Parker's "journalistic ambitions."

———. *Theodore Parker*. Boston: Little, Brown and Company, 1936. Although this most recent biography is crowded with names and references, it is highly readable. Since the documentation is supplied only chapter by chapter, individual facts and quotations can be traced only with difficulty.

COOKE, GEORGE WILLIS. *Unitarianism in America*. Boston: American Unitarian Association, 1902, Standard history; author sympathetic to the Transcendentalists.

DICKS, JOHN EDWARD. *The Critical Theology of Theodore Parker*. New York: Columbia University Press, 1948. Excellent study of Parker's theology and its background. The Levi Blodgett letter is reprinted on pp. 137-60.

EMERSON, RALPH WALDO. *Works*. Boston: Houghton, Mifflin Company, 1883.

FAUST, CLARENCE H. "The Background of the Unitarian Opposition to Transcendentalism," *Modern Philology*, XXV (1937), 297-324. Indispensable.

FROTHINGHAM, O. B. *Recollections and Impressions, 1822-1890*.

New York: G. P. Putnam's Sons, 1891. This autobiographical work contains many informed remarks on Parker and remains one of the best accounts of liberal Christianity in the nineteenth century.

————. *Theodore Parker*. Boston: James R. Osgood and Company, 1874. Still the best biography, this is the only source for some of the facts about Parker. Frothingham knew Parker and, here and in other books, has provided much of our information about Parker, his contemporaries and their controversies.

————. *Transcendentalism in New England*. New York: G. P. Putnam's Sons, 1876. The chapter on Parker in this very uneven book contributes little to the understanding of the man.

GODDARD, HAROLD CLARKE. *Studies in New England Transcendentalism*. New York: Columbia University Press, 1908. Essential reading for anyone studying Transcendentalism, but the books adds little to the material on Parker in the biographies.

GOHDES, CLARENCE. *The Periodicals of American Transcendentalism*. Durham, N.C.: Duke University Press, 1931. The best account of Parker's *Massachusetts Quarterly Review* as a periodical of the movement.

HAROUTUNIAN, JOSEPH. *Piety versus Moralism*. New York: Henry Holt and Company, 1932. Excellent analysis of the Unitarian separation from Congregationalism in the chapter "The Unitarian Revolt."

LADU, ARTHUR I. "The Political Ideas of Theodore Parker," *Studies in Philology,* XXXVIII (1941), 106-23. Demonstrates that Parker's political ideas are those of most of the other Transcendentalists.

LEVY, LEONARD W. "Sims' Case: The Fugitive Slave Law in Boston," *Journal of Negro History,* XXXV (1950), 39-74.

LEWIS, R. W. B. *The American Adam*. Chicago: University of Chicago Press, 1955. Lewis mitigate the importance of Parker's contribution to theology but emphasizes the view of man Parker held: "every individual was in spirit and in fact a perfectly new man."

MARTIN, JOHN H. "Theodore Parker" Ph.D. dissertation (University of Chicago, 1953). The most thorough, orderly and detailed presentation of Parker's biography.

MEAD, DAVID. *Yankee Eloquence in the Middle West: The Ohio Lyceum 1850-1870*. East Lansing, Mich.: Michigan State College Press, 1951. Account of Parker's lectures in Ohio based on newspaper reports and on Parker's manuscript Lyceum Diary.

NELSON, TRUMAN. *The Passion by the Brook.* Garden City, N.Y.: Doubleday and Company, 1953. Fictional account of Brook Farm, with much attention to Parker.

————. *The Sin of the Prophet.* Boston: Little, Brown and Company, 1952. The author of this fictional account of Parker and Anthony Burns studied Parker for more years and with more care than any other scholar; hence the novel must be considered one of the significant interpretations of Parker.

NEWBROUGH, GEORGE F. "Reason and Understanding in the Works of Theodore Parker," *South Atlantic Quarterly,* XLVII (1948), 64-75.

PARRINGTON, VERNON L. *Main Currents in American Thought.* New York: Harcourt, Brace and Company, 1927. In his section on Parker, "Theodore Parker: Transcendental Minister," Parrington describes him as "one of the greatest, if not the last, of the excellent line of Puritan preachers," but the emphasis is on Parker as a political critic.

PERSONS, STOW. *Free Religion, An American Faith.* New Haven: Yale University Press, 1947. A description and history of the religious movements that were, to a degree, the results of Parker's efforts in theology.

POCHMANN, HENRY A. *German Culture in America: Philosophical and Literary Influences, 1600-1900.* Madison, Wis.: University of Wisconsin Press, 1957. An excellent short account of Parker's debt to German thought and his contribution to American religion. Pp. 215-22.

RIBACK, WILLIAM H. "Theodore Parker of Boston: Social Reformer." *Social Service Review,* XXII (1948), 451-60. The best review of Parker's social efforts. Contains a discussion of the way in which Parker had to work in order to avoid hurting a cause by having his name associated with it.

SHAPIRO, SAMUEL. "The Rendition of Anthony Burns," *Journal of Negro History,* XLIV (1959), 34-51. Best account of the series of events.

SMITH, H. SHELTON. "Was Theodore Parker a Transcendentalist?" *New England Quarterly,* XXIII (1950), 351-64. A reply to Commager's "The Dilemma of Theodore Parker."

WEISS, JOHN. *Life and Correspondence of Theodcre Parker.* 2 vols. New York: D. Appleton and Co., 1864. This very lengthy work contains invaluable material for the study of Theodore Parker and his work. Unfortunately, the virtual lack of organization makes it almost impossible to use.

WELLEK, RENE. "The Minor Transcendentalists and German Philosophy." *New England Quarterly,* XV (1942), 652-80. Claims that Jacobi and Schleiermacher are more important to the Transcendentalists than Kant and Hegel.

Index